You Can Teach Improv (Yes, You!)

The Ultimate Guide to Class Planning, Skill Building, and Helping Every Student Leave With a Win

Andrew Berkowitz

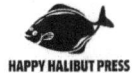

HAPPY HALIBUT PRESS

To Pat and Ruth.
A lot is not wrong with my life because of you.

In learning you will teach and in teaching you will learn.

— Phil Collins

Su-su-ssudio oh oh.

— Phil Collins

Contents

Chapter 1
Welcome to Teaching

I still remember teaching my first improv class.

I had just completed a four-year university program in improvisational education theory, followed by two years of supervised student teaching. Now, with hundreds of hours of applied pedagogy under my belt, I inhaled one deep, calming breath and confidently strode into the classroom. This was the moment I had been training for. I felt completely at peace, prepared to help my students begin their improv journey.

Just kidding!

In reality, I was *wildly* unprepared to teach my first improv class: I found out that I would be the instructor just two days beforehand. My only "qualifications" were that I was available on a Wednesday night at 7 p.m. And if you'd asked me what a *syllabus* was, I would have guessed an STD.

My first class as a teacher was a mess—but it was also a lot of fun. My students didn't run screaming from the class. I came away from the experience excited and energized. Maybe some people even learned something. Emboldened, I came back to teach again.

Eventually, through trial and error, I learned how to teach improv. In fact, over the past twenty-five years, I've discovered that I love teaching just as much as I love improvising. And that's why I wrote this book.

Because many people have a similarly rough start when they begin teaching improv. Oftentimes, they are thrown into the classroom with little or no training, selected to teach only because they're a talented improviser, they volunteered, or because they are literally the only person available on Wednesday night at 7 p.m.

This is the book I wish I'd had when I began my improv teaching journey. It guides you through the fundamentals of good instruction. You'll learn how to choose a class topic, plan your curriculum, run exercises, keep your class flowing, side coach, and handle all kinds of students. It's everything you need to successfully plan and teach your first class.

Will reading this book make you a great teacher overnight? Nope. But it *will* give you a solid foundation so you can start off your teaching journey on the right foot. Just like learning to improvise, you'll need practice for your skills to grow as a teacher. My hope is that this book will point you in the right direction, so you keep coming back to teach again and again.

Ready? Let's go!

What This Book Is

This book is for anyone who is interested in starting to teach improv, or in improving their teaching skills. Improvisation is a lifetime journey, and we are always learning and growing. At festivals, it's common to see headlining performers taking classes alongside new students, just to learn new perspectives. My hope is that wherever you are in your improv and teaching journey, this book will help open your eyes to new possibilities.

Sprinkled throughout the book, you'll read anecdotes from improvisers who were kind enough to share stories about how great teachers changed their lives.

What This Book Isn't

Before we get started, you should know that there are a few things I will *not* cover in this book:

- **This is not a book about how to improvise.** I'll assume you have previous experience with improv and you're familiar with basic scenework, games, and improvisational structure. By no means do you need to be an advanced improviser to use this book (or to teach an improv class), but if you've *never* improvised before, you'll probably want to take a class or two before diving in.

- **This is not a book of improv exercises.** There are many other books and online resources where you can find specific improv exercises and even entire curricula. (I point you to some of those resources in the companion website.) This book teaches you how to create your own exercises and how to incorporate existing exercises into your own curriculum; it's not a specific syllabus for you to copy.

- **This book focuses on teaching adults (or at least, adult-like humans).** If you own or operate kids, you can probably figure out how to take the information in this book and apply it to youth.

- **This is not a book about directing a show or leading an ensemble.** We'll specifically focus on planning and executing an individual improv class or class series. If you've been tasked with coaching a group, leading a team, or directing a show, that's beyond the scope of this book. For help with that, check out some recommended resources at youcanteachimprov.com.

You Are Qualified to Teach

Before we jump into the good stuff, let's address the number one question I get when I encourage people to start teaching:

"AM I EVEN QUALIFIED TO TEACH IMPROV?"

YES!

The biggest factor holding people back from starting to teach is the belief that they are not qualified. Either they think they don't yet have enough improv experience to lead a class, or they believe that they aren't a good enough improviser. Both beliefs are misguided.

You don't need years and years of experience to be a qualified teacher. Did you know that most people become flight instructors soon after they learn to fly? As long as you understand the fundamentals of the skill you are teaching—and more importantly, can break that skill down into smaller exercises—you are perfectly qualified. In fact, you may even find it *easier* to teach some skills because you more recently went through your own learning process. You still remember what it was like to be a student learning that skill.

As for whether you are a good enough improviser to be a teacher, let me be blunt:

THERE IS LITTLE CORRELATION BETWEEN IMPROV SKILL AND TEACHING SKILL.

Improvising and teaching are two completely separate disciplines. I've taken fantastic classes from so-so improvisers who happen to be great teachers. I've taken dreadful "master classes" from famous improvisers who happen to be bad teachers.

If you think that you aren't a talented enough improviser to become a teacher, think again. Your success in the classroom will be based on your abilities as a *teacher*, not as an improviser.

So, Why Teach Improv?

Because you picked up this book, I'll assume you're already interested in teaching improv. Here are some additional reasons—beyond initial interest—that show just how beneficial teaching improv can be:

You Become a Better Performer

Effective teaching is all about deconstructing how improv works. You'll have to figure out how to break essential skills into their component parts and then create exercises to help students master those parts—or overcome blockers that get in their way. By doing this kind of analysis, you'll learn to see improv in a whole new light and gain a much deeper understanding of the parts that make up the whole.

Similarly, the act of observing students, identifying problems, and making corrections will train you to see improv through a more alert set of eyes. Improv is primarily about listening, observing, and reacting—and teaching gives you hours of practice doing just that.

Every successful teacher I've known has simultaneously become a better performer. It's a happy by-product of learning to teach.

You Learn to Solve Your Own Improv Problems

Once you learn to effectively teach others, you can also apply those teaching skills to yourself. Everybody has gaps in their skill set or occasionally goes through a slump where it feels like they can't do anything right. With teaching experience, you'll find it easier to be self-reflective and diagnose what you need to do to improve your craft.

You Get to Give Back to Your Team

There are few things more satisfying than helping a student make a breakthrough. Whether you're teaching an introductory class where students are just barely getting over their fear of being on stage or an advanced class where students are whizzing through complex structures and formats, that instant where someone has an "a-ha moment" is incredibly fulfilling to witness.

You already know how much improv has changed you for the better. I bet there's a teacher who made a meaningful difference in your own improv journey and in your life. Now you have the opportunity to do the same for others. Trust me when I tell you that it will be deeply, deeply rewarding.

> *A big breakthrough happened for me after this note from the teacher: "I see you drop your ideas completely and go along with whatever someone else comes in with." I realized this was a very Amber habit and improv could be the tool to help me better connect and collaborate with others on- and off-stage.*
>
> — Amber Pedersen

It Opens Doors to Meet New Friends and to Travel

As a teacher, you not only get to meet new people in your own classes, but you can also travel to teach at workshops and festivals in other cities—and even other countries. Teaching as a guest instructor with another troupe, or as a guest teacher at an improv festival, puts you in an exclusive club that can enrich your life and your improv career. Teaching has introduced me to lifelong friends and afforded me the opportunity to travel the world, sharing my knowledge with others.

It's So Much Fun

As you'll learn from this book, teaching is its own kind of performance. You are "on" from the moment you walk through the door, responsible for guiding, inspiring, challenging, and entertaining your students for the entire class. I find teaching as invigorating (and exhausting) as doing a performance. If you're doing it right, it should feel as satisfying as putting on a show. It's that much fun!

Chapter 2
What Makes a Great Teacher

Every teacher has a unique style and persona, just like every improviser has their own flair and stage presence. Over time, you will develop your own teaching persona—ideally one that is authentic to you and connects effectively with your students. While teaching styles are unique, all great improv teachers share key attributes that lead to their success as instructors:

Well-Organized, Written Lesson Plans

A great teacher comes into every class with a complete, written syllabus and a solid plan for how the class time will be spent. From warm-ups to exercises to reflection, they have a roadmap of activities for each session. They know exactly what their goals are and have laid out exercises in a specific order. They're never just "winging it" or making it up as they go along.

This doesn't mean that they won't adjust and make changes over the course of the class. In fact, planning extra content and accounting for curriculum adjustments is something I recommend (more on that in chapter 7). But even knowing that they may, well, *improvise* during the class, a great teacher comes in with a well-organized, written plan.

Efficient Class Management

A great teacher runs a smooth, organized class. Students feel as though the teacher is in control from the moment they walk through the door until departing for post-workshop drinks. Running an efficient class encompasses everything from time management to structuring the flow of exercises to handling questions—and even navigating the individual needs of different students.

Great teachers also focus on stage time, striving to talk less and give students more opportunities to practice.

As a teacher, you are the director of the class, and you should feel comfortably in control. Managing ten to twenty students (or more) is not an easy task, and we'll talk much more about this in later chapters.

Enthusiasm and Energy

A great class has an energy about it.

The students are excited, the room is buzzing, and the transitions from exercise to exercise feel seamless. Even when doing slower, more thoughtful work, you can *feel* that people are having breakthroughs. They are learning, discovering, and being challenged.

They are fully engaged.

As a teacher, it's your job to drive this energy. You must always project a sense of excitement and enthusiasm for the work. You want the students to truly believe that in this moment, there is nowhere else you would want to be.

Inspiring and Motivating Guidance

Some students may be in your class because they consider improv a true art form and aspire to be professional actors. Others may have signed up because their spouse told them to get out of the house. No matter what their original motivation was, your job is to inspire.

You already know how improv has changed your life for the better. As a teacher, your mission is to help your students feel that same sense of inspiration. When you are unrelentingly enthusiastic about the possibilities that improv brings—and what you have to teach during class time—your students will share that attitude.

> *Rich Talarico spoke about the joy of discovery, and how it's so much more fulfilling to discover something together in a scene than to strong-arm an idea to completion. The way he put it was awesome: "It's the difference between building a fire with a flamethrower versus rubbing two sticks together." I quote that all the time, and I think it's a great metaphor for all aspects of life—it's amazing what happens when we collaborate!*
>
> — Sara Grossbarth

Constructive and Kind Criticism

As a teacher, you walk a fine line between helping people learn and grow, and correcting, adjusting, and even critiquing their performance. It's critical that you do this with a positive attitude so redirection from bad habits to good habits feels uplifting and encouraging. You should endeavor to make students feel successful and celebrate small victories as huge wins. When you do have to correct or criticize, you should do it in a supportive manner so that students understand they are not doing something "wrong," but have new ideas and opportunities for more success on stage.

Candor and Honest Feedback

Most of your students want to improve, whether that means joining the mainstage company, succeeding in an audition, or just feeling more success in scenes. You won't do students any favors if you can't be candid with them.

Being candid means telling students—honestly—what they do well *and* where the gaps are in their performance. You can't help students by withholding feedback when they need it.

Every student requires a different level of candor depending on their goals and where they are in their improv journey. Learning to deliver candid feedback is one of the harder skills to develop as an instructor, but it is essential to running a successful class for both teacher and student.

Demanding

Students want to be challenged. If your classes are too easy or you refuse to side coach or correct errors, you're not doing your job.

Being demanding does not mean you make your classes too hard or that you push students beyond their abilities. It doesn't mean that you shout at or belittle your students. It does mean that you take students just past their current abilities into the zone where they are learning. You actively insist that they do their best work instead of letting them get away with sloppy choices. You insist that they play at the top of their intelligence.

Students thrive when the teacher demands the best of them.

Empathy and Safe Environments

Improv is challenging, scary, and emotional for many people. New students are often terrified just being in the room. Even more experienced students can be intimidated by their peers or uncomfortable showing the vulnerability required in honest scenework. Great improv scenes can be deeply emotional. As those emotions are revealed on stage, you'll see the doubts, fears, and hesitancies of your students revealed.

As a teacher, you must provide empathy, understanding, and flexibility to meet your students where they are and to guide them through a successful class. It is also your responsibility to create and enforce a safe environment. That means setting physical, verbal, and content boundaries right at the beginning of class and addressing any issues should they arise. If you're guiding students through difficult or challenging work, make sure you have their consent and let them know that they have the power to stop any exercise if it strays outside of their comfort zone.

Now that we've reviewed the attributes that make a successful teacher, let's dive into the actual teaching. We'll start—as you should—with planning your curriculum.

Chapter 3
Choosing Your Class Topic

L et's make a plan!

Putting together a detailed and thoughtful syllabus —including topic, warm-ups, skills, exercises, and reflections—is the first step to teaching a great class. Too many teachers shortchange this step of the process, picking overly broad or unfocused class topics, neglecting to think through the individual component skills that students will need to learn, or failing to design exercises that build upon one another in logical steps.

In the next few chapters, we're going to walk step-by-step through everything you need to design a killer class. By the end, you'll have the tools to identify a well-focused class topic, break that topic into individual skills, and develop exercises that help students see progress by the end of the session.

Most importantly, we're going to teach you to create your own exercises if you wish, rather than relying on exercises you've done before or taken from a pre-written curriculum. Once you have developed this ability, you'll be a better, more confident teacher—and a better improviser. You'll be able to deconstruct and learn *any* improv skill, even those that you're still acquiring yourself.

It all starts with choosing a class topic.

How to Pick a Topic

Choosing the topic for your class is the first and most important step in creating your syllabus. Selecting a narrowly focused, well-defined topic will allow you to craft a syllabus that gives students recognizable results by the end of the class. We've all been to classes where it wasn't clear what the teacher was trying to accomplish or what the point of the instruction was.

Here are some examples of topics that are too broad:

- Scenework
- Music
- Character
- Genre
- Narrative

There are literally *dozens* of different skills you could work on within any of these topics. If you go into a single class determined to tackle "Scenework" or "Character" you're going to end up with an unfocused class and confused students.

Overly broad class topics aren't the only problem. Sometimes teachers pick class topics that are overly vague. In these classes, the teacher *sort of* has an idea about what they're interested in exploring, but they never make it concrete enough that the students understand the point. Here are some examples of overly vague class topics:

- Connection
- Feeling
- Nature
- Discovery
- Intuition

Contained within each of these buzzwords may be something (or likely, many things) well worth exploring, but until the teacher focuses and defines the true goal, there's real danger of creating a class that achieves little and leaves students baffled. Let me be clear: there's nothing wrong with these topics when used as the *inspiration* for your class. But that's all they should be—inspiration. To create a compelling, focused, and successful class, you'll need to be very specific about what you're actually seeking to accomplish. This is where the hard work of focus and definition begins. The best way to do that is to create a thesis.

Creating a Thesis for Your Class

The class thesis defines the problem you are trying to solve, why it matters, and what success will look like at the end of the class. A well-defined thesis will be your road map as you begin to break down individual skills and exercises. It will allow you to communicate clearly to your students what your class is about and exactly what they should expect to achieve.

A good class thesis has three components:

- A (specific) problem.
- Why that problem matters.
- What success looks like.

Let's look at an example:

- **Specific problem:** Scenes are having a lot of arguments and negotiations.
- **Why that problem matters:** The scene gets stuck and nothing advances.
- **What success looks like:** Dynamic scenes where the improvisers are in agreement and the narrative moves forward.

Here's one from a short-form troupe:

- **Specific problem:** In character-switch games, performers aren't playing well-defined characters.
- **Why that problem matters:** Since the point of the game is to embody other performers' characters, there's nothing to embody and the gimmick of the game falls flat.
- **What success looks like:** Actors play very specific characters that are easy for others to model, and the game is successful.

Here's one from the world of musical improv:

- **Specific problem:** In musical games, the performers appear to lack confidence.
- **Why that problem matters:** The actors don't look or sound very good to the audience. Because of the lukewarm audience reaction, improvisers feel reluctant to play musical games.
- **What success looks like:** Actors feel confident in their singing and wow the audience with their musical skills.

And one more:

- **Specific problem:** Scenes lack stakes.
- **Why that problem matters:** Nothing interesting happens in the scene and the audience doesn't care about the characters.
- **What success looks like:** Scenes are full of rich stakes where the audience is invested in what happens.

Notice that each of these theses is much more specific than "Scenework," or "Character," or "Music." We have closely defined a *specific problem* that is impacting performance and clearly described what success looks like.

In describing your thesis for the class, it can be helpful to start with the phrase, "I've noticed...":

- **I've noticed ...** that our short-form scenes all take place in one location at a single point in time and we don't use edits the way we do in long-form scenes.

- **I've noticed ...** that when real emotions arise during an Armando, the performers often make a joke or deflect instead of following the emotion.

- **I've noticed ...** that in our verbal clue-giving games we are either too obvious or not obvious enough, so the game either ends too soon or goes on for too long.

Your "I've noticed..." statement doesn't just have to be something you've noticed in your team or troupe. It can also be something you've noticed *in general* for students at their level:

- **I've noticed ...** that 101-level students often get stuck in scenes that are about doing an activity instead of about emotions or relationships.

- **I've noticed ...** that 201-level students often play at the center of the stage instead of exploring the space.

- **I've noticed ...** that performers in our student shows play at a much slower pace than players in our mainstage cast.

Once you've described the specific problem that you've noticed, you can use it to develop the remaining parts of your thesis.

One caution: even using this technique, it's still easy to accidentally create a topic for your class that is too broad. For instance, you could easily say things like: "I've noticed that our scenework is not very good" or "I've noticed that our musical games are not successful." To avoid these overly broad topics and determine if our thesis is specific enough, you need to use the "Why Technique."

Visit youcanteachimprov.com to download a worksheet for creating your thesis.

Testing Your Thesis with the "Why Technique"

Use the "Why Technique" to dig deeper and determine if your thesis is specific enough for a class. Here's how it works: for any thesis, write down all the reasons *why* students have that specific problem. Below, I've applied the "Why Technique" to an earlier thesis example.

Specific problem: I've noticed that 201-level students are often stuck playing at the center of the stage instead of exploring the space. *Why?*

- Nobody has ever told them they can use more of the stage, so they've never practiced that.
- During previous classes, they never had any chairs or stools on stage, so they always stood.
- They have been coached that they should never turn their backs on the audience.

It feels as though these reasons why can be addressed in a single improv class.

Now let's look at another thesis example, this time with a topic ("music") that is *too broad*:

Specific problem: I've noticed that our musical games are not successful. *Why?*

- We often panic-sing as soon as the music starts instead of waiting out the intro and finding the keyboard player's tempo and key.
- We are fearful of singing so we sing quietly.
- We are trying to rhyme everything, so our songs are either nonsensical or we get flustered when we can't rhyme.
- When we do rhyme, we exclusively use an AAAA or AABB rhyme scheme instead of an easier ABCB rhyme scheme.
- We don't know how to set a chorus, so songs meander for a long time.
- We don't know how to find an ending, so songs go on for too long or just peter out.

- We don't sell the song with our stage presence.
- We try to sing too many words instead of leaving pauses or singing in half-time.

And so on...

There's no way you could attack all of these reasons in a single class. A very long list of challenges is a tip-off that your topic is WAY too broad for one session. Instead, take one or two of these "Whys" and use those for a more focused thesis problem. A more specific and improved thesis problem could be:

- **Specific problem:** I've noticed that we struggle with rhyming in our music games.

Or...

- **Specific Problem:** I've noticed that we lack confidence in singing so we sing quietly and with poor stage presence.

Or...

- **Specific Problem:** I've noticed that we haven't learned to chorus.

From there, we can build a class around the more-focused, three-part thesis:

- **Specific problem:** We are not creating choruses in our musical games.
- **Why that problem matters:** Our songs meander on for a long time and never find a big ending.

- **What success looks like:** Our musical numbers feel like real songs and have powerful, audience-pleasing choruses.

Building a class around chorusing feels focused and achievable. You'll be able to define for the students *exactly* what the goal is and what success looks like. Remember: it's hard to have a class topic that is too focused, but it's very easy to plan a class that's too broad. When you try to solve too many problems in a single class, students will leave uninspired and without any big wins.

Avoiding Vague Topics

Earlier we said that not only are overly broad topics a problem for planning your class, but so are overly *vague* topics. Things like:

- Connection
- Feeling
- Nature
- Discovery
- Intuition

Sometimes we get caught up in buzzwords like these that *sound* sexy, but it's critical that we dig deeper to uncover what we *really* mean and what tangible, describable, achievable problems and outcomes we can define. Otherwise, we run the risk of presenting a class with no specific point, nothing for students to grasp onto, and ultimately little value.

You've probably been in such classes before, especially at improv festivals where you get navel-gazing class descriptions like, *"In this session we're going to explore the space between consciousness and technology, inspired by nature and finding the small monsters that live inside all of us."*

WTF?

Wrangling Vague Topics

Use the "I've noticed…" technique to determine if a topic contains an actual definable problem, or is simply too ineffable. It may take some introspection to ask yourself what you're *really* getting at:

> *"Discovery … what do I mean by discovery? When I do improv I love the fact that I get to play characters or situations that are different from the real me. In fact, I get to feel brave on stage trying on personas that I would never be in real life."*

Okay, we're getting closer. We've defined what discovery means to us, but we still haven't defined a problem that we can attach a thesis to. Let's dig deeper:

> *"I feel like I often take the safe route in scenes, shying away from characters who are against my nature. I end up playing vanilla scenes about real life instead of exploring exotic jobs, locations, or situations. Why am I always making myself the dad in scenes set at home instead of a pirate on a 17th-century ship or a penguin biologist in the Antarctic?"*

Getting closer! Now let's turn this into an "I've noticed…" problem:

I've noticed ... that I often play characters that are similar to real-life me instead of playing wildly different and exotic characters.

And let's play the "Why Game":

I often play characters that are similar to real-life me. Why?

- I play my characters without enough commitment, feeling embarrassed that it's "me" playing a pirate instead of "being" a pirate.
- I take scene suggestions literally instead of using them as a springboard.
- I've never had a chance to practice this in a class.

Sounds like a manageable number of Whys! Can we turn this into a thesis statement? I bet we can:

- **Specific problem:** We usually play characters that are close versions of our own lives.
- **Why that problem matters:** We end up in a lot of the same, mundane scenes again and again, and don't stretch as improvisers or find variety in our shows.
- **What success looks like:** We play exotic characters in unique locations and situations, giving both the audience and ourselves a sense of adventure and wonder.

Although topics like "Discovery" and "Connection" sound intriguing in the abstract, once you dive deeper it's clear that you have to define the specific problems you're looking to solve and the specific outcomes that the performers will achieve. Be relentless in asking yourself what you *really* mean and use "I've noticed" and the "Why Technique" until you narrow your topic down to something that is focused and tangible.

Even if you feel like being experimental, your experiment will be far more successful if you can define the problem, why it matters, and what success looks like.

> *After our last class with TJ Jagadowski, several of us went to get a drink at a nearby bar. TJ asked us all to go around the table and tell him about ourselves and how we came to be doing improv in Chicago. So, I told my story about how I was from New Orleans and such. Over a year later, I ran into him waiting for a train. Katrina had happened several months prior, and TJ asked me if my family was okay. He had genuinely listened at that bar table on that day after class and remembered all that, and cared enough to ask about my family. Listening, remembering, and caring makes you a better teacher.*
>
> — Chip Aucoin

Chapter 4
Identifying Atomic Skills

N ow that you've picked a topic for your class, one that is just the right size (not too broad, not too narrow) and easily defined by a thesis statement, you know exactly what problem you're looking to solve, why it matters, and what success will look like at the end of the class.

Your next step is to take the outcome you're looking to achieve and break it down into the "atomic skills" necessary for success.

> **IMPORTANT: SKILLS ARE NOT THE SAME THING AS EXERCISES. EXERCISES ARE HOW YOU LEARN A SKILL; SKILLS ARE THE ACTUAL BUILDING BLOCKS. IT'S A MISTAKE TO LEAP DIRECTLY FROM CLASS TOPIC TO EXERCISES WITHOUT FIRST CONSIDERING THE NECESSARY SKILLS.**

- **Skill:** Building character through physicality.
- **Exercise:** Character walk.

- **Skill:** Sharing the focus in scenework.
- **Exercise:** Performer must move on stage before speaking.

- **Skill:** Using "third thought" inspiration from audience suggestions.
- **Exercise:** Do five scene starts from one suggestion.

Always start with skills, *then* consider exercises: to learn skill X, students will do exercise Y.

What Are Atomic Skills?

Everything we do in improv is composed of smaller building blocks that come together to form a whole. As a teacher, it's your job to figure out what those building blocks are. You then create a curriculum that starts with the most foundational block, and then continues by stacking one block upon another until you reach the desired goal. These building blocks are called *atomic skills*, and they're the key to helping students learn efficiently.

To see atomic skills in action, imagine you are taking a guitar class. On your first day of class, the teacher doesn't just hand you a guitar and tell you to start playing songs.

- First you learn how to hold the guitar.
- Next, you learn how to strum the strings while holding the guitar.
- Then you learn how to form a chord while holding and strumming the guitar.
- You progress to changing from one chord to another while holding and strumming the guitar.

- Finally, the teacher has you play a simple two-chord song (probably "Achy Breaky Heart").

In this example, each skill builds upon the previous one. You'd never be asked to play a song before you even learned to hold the guitar!

Unfortunately, improv teachers often neglect these atomic skills and instead leap right into "play the song!" Perhaps you've been in improv classes before where the teacher simply described the desired outcome (what success looks like) and then immediately got students up to perform with that end goal in mind. I once took a class where the goal was to "do better object work." The teacher described what he meant by "better" object work and then we got up on stage to start playing scenes. This was not successful, because we hadn't yet learned any of the necessary skills. The teacher should have broken down object work into each of the atomic skill building blocks and stacked them one on top of another.

Let's try this now!

How to Identify Atomic Skills

Think about all the skills that go into doing object work. Which are the most foundational? Which skills must stack on top of each other (in other words, you can't do B until you've learned to do A)? Give it a few moments of thought and jot down your answers. When you're ready, turn the page to compare your answers.

Here are some stackable atomic skills for object work:

- Showing the shape of an object.
- Showing the weight of an object.
- Picking up and using objects, showing shape and weight.
- Defining objects that are fixed in the space, like furniture, doors, and walls.
- Moving around a space where objects have been defined.
- Keeping a scene going while using objects.
- Keeping a scene going while using objects and navigating the physical space.

Each of these individual skills stacks upon the previous one. You can't pick up and use an object until you've learned to define its shape and weight. You can't move around a space with fixed objects unless someone has defined those objects in the space. And you can't do a scene with object and space work until you've learned to define those objects and the space.

How did you do? Don't worry if your answers didn't exactly match the above example. It takes practice to think in terms of atomic skills. And every teacher is going to come up with a different approach. There's no "right" way to break up skills (or to teach improv!).

Let's try another one. Remember this thesis from earlier:

- **Specific problem:** In character-switch games, performers aren't playing well-defined characters.
- **Why that problem matters:** Since the point of the game is to embody other performers' characters,

there's nothing to embody and the gimmick of the game falls flat.

- **What success looks like:** Actors play very specific characters that are easy for others to model and the game is successful.

Think about how you might break this into atomic skills. What are the basic components of creating an easily recognized character? How would you introduce a character-switch game? How would you stack skills in order to make such a game successful? Remember, we're defining *skills* here; exercises will come later.

Jot down a list of atomic skills and when you're ready, turn the page to compare your answers.

Here are some stackable atomic skills for creating well-defined characters and succeeding in a character-switch game:

- Using voice to create a recognizable character.
- Using posture to create a recognizable character.
- Using movement to create a recognizable character.
- Using multiple attributes (for instance, voice *and* posture) to create a character.
- Copying one attribute of someone else's character.
- Heightening one attribute of someone else's character.
- Copying all attributes of someone else's character.
- Heightening all attributes of someone else's character.
- Keeping a scene going while assuming someone else's character.
- Keeping a scene going while assuming and heightening someone else's character.

My thought process behind the above example:

- First, you have to give students tools to create recognizable characters—perhaps using voice, posture, and physicality.
- Then, you want students to achieve the skill of copying someone else's character.
- To keep it bite-sized and atomic, students should first practice copying just *one* attribute of someone else's character (perhaps just their voice or just their physicality) before stacking another skill on top and copying everything.
- Next, students should work on the skill of not just matching someone else's character, but *heightening* it.

- Finally, students should practice the skill of keeping a scene going after they've switched into someone else's character.

Did you come up with a different approach? It's fine if you did! Building skills incrementally like this helps students practice each component of the game in bite-sized pieces. Each building block is small enough to be a simple addition to the last thing they just learned.

Smaller Is Better!

Students can really only focus on *one* thing at a time. Each atomic skill should be a single thing that builds upon previous skills. It should also be something that you can quickly explain and demonstrate.

If it takes you more than a couple of sentences to explain what success looks like—or if there is more than one thing for the student to focus on during the exercise—this is a tip-off that you haven't broken down the thesis into small enough atomic skills.

In the character-switch example above, you can easily explain the jump from using posture to using movement by saying:

> *"Now that you've learned to create a character through posture, we're going to keep that posture and add movement around the stage to make your character more dynamic."*

Success was explained in a single sentence, and it involved adding just one additional skill atop the skill students had just learned.

But what would happen if I skipped a few steps and tried to jump from creating character through posture to heightening *all* the attributes of someone's character? My instructions might sound something like:

> *"Now that you've learned to create a character through posture, we're going to practice copying everything about someone else's character and then heightening. You'll copy posture, but also pay attention to their voice, their point of view, and their movement around the stage. Make sure you heighten as well. This means take everything you see and do it bigger or more specifically."*

[Sound of heads exploding.]

We've added not one but *many* skills here. Students have just learned to create a character through posture, but now we're asking them to add in voice and point of view, to copy someone else's character, and to heighten. Chances are they would struggle to put all of those skills together, some of which they haven't learned yet.

The beautiful thing about making your atomic skills super small is that you can move through them quickly if students are getting it. Should you discover that your students have no trouble creating recognizable characters through voice, attitude, and/or posture, you can quickly move on to copying, heightening, and sustaining a scene.

Let's break one more class topic into atomic skills, just to lock in this concept:

- **Specific problem:** Our scenes lack stakes.
- **Why that problem matters:** Nothing interesting happens in the scene and we don't care about the characters.
- **What success looks like:** Scenes are full of rich stakes where we are invested in what happens.

How would you break this into atomic skills? Jot down your answers and when you're ready, turn the page.

Here are some atomic skills for creating scenes with high stakes:

- Listening for an offer.
- Agreeing with the offer that was presented.
- Heightening the offer.
- Making it personal and showing how the offer affects the character.
- Making it meaningful and showing how the offer affects the character *and* is important.
- Making it meaningful to *both* characters.
- Keeping the stakes high throughout the scene.

My thought process:

- The foundational skill for most scenework is making and hearing offers. You want to make sure that students are listening to each other as a base skill.
- Next, you need to ensure that students are in agreement. Without agreement, they'll fall into an argument or negotiation and have trouble focusing the scene.
- Once the students are on the same page, they'll need to heighten. This is where the stakes come in.
- After students have heightened, they need to know how and why it affects a character. If the story doesn't impact any characters, the audience won't care.
- Not only does a character need to be affected, but they need to be *deeply* affected. If it's no big deal to them, it will be no big deal to the audience.
- Ideally, in a two-person scene, both characters will be deeply affected. If a scene is only important to one

character, you run the risk of the characters
negotiating the stakes instead of plunging forward.

- Finally, you want to make sure that the characters
continue to heighten and drive the story forward,
rather than lowering the stakes by solving the
problem.

Did you have similar answers? Maybe you came up with even
smaller skills—that's fine, too! The key is to make each skill
simple, discreet, achievable, and stackable.

Don't worry if you feel your listed skills may need some adjustment. Our next task will be to develop exercises to learn and
practice each atomic skill. As you create these exercises, you'll
discover whether you need to adjust or combine your atomic
skills.

Ready? Let's go build some exercises!

Chapter 5
Developing Exercises

Now that you have your list of atomic skills, it's time to develop exercises to teach each skill. Each exercise should be simple to describe, understand, and accomplish. If you've made the skills small enough, it should be straightforward to come up with exercises.

For teaching any skill you have two options: use an existing exercise or invent your own.

Using Existing Exercises

Let's say the atomic skill you want to teach is:

- *Using movement to form a character.*

This sounds like a character walk exercise, and I'll bet that you've already been in several improv classes—maybe *many* improv classes—that have done character walks. Absolutely feel free to pick an exercise you've done before. You do not have to reinvent the wheel, and you should not feel guilty about using an exercise you're familiar with. Improv exercises are not copyrighted!

There are plentiful resources on the internet to find improv exercises that teach specific skills (see this book's companion site for links). Veteran teachers in your troupe can share their favorite exercises, or you can ask in any improv teachers group on Facebook to get scads of ideas.

If you're using an exercise from another teacher or from an online resource, remember that just because someone else developed an exercise or a syllabus doesn't mean that it has been totally thought through and will work for your students. Before you try an exercise in your class, make sure you know why you're doing it, what specific skill it's designed to teach, and what success looks like. Feel free to modify the exercise to better fit what you're trying to teach, or to improve on the original.

Borrowing Entire Classes

It's common to take a terrific class at a festival (or at another theater) and want to bring it back to teach to your own team. Sometimes the teacher you took the class from will even generously share their syllabus with you.

When you do borrow from someone else's class, be sure to give credit and then make it your own. You should not try to copy their class exactly. Change exercises or explanations to match the needs of your students and to play to your strengths as a teacher. Add or remove anything as you see fit.

Try to avoid saying things like: "This is how we learned it in the class" or "The teacher said you should..." This is your own unique teaching experience! Instead, you can say something like, "Today we're going to work on solo scenes, inspired by a class I took from Bethany Garner at the Rock Island Improv Festival." Then put *your* unique spin on the class.

Keep in mind that it's not cool to take another teacher's syllabus and try to pass it off as your own without giving credit, and it's *definitely* not OK to take another teacher's syllabus and charge money for the class. If you're charging money, develop your own syllabus, or even better hire the original teacher to come teach at your theater.

Inventing Your Own Exercises

You should also feel free to invent your own exercises. There's nobody better than you to perfectly develop an exercise for the skill you're teaching. Don't feel shy about creating exactly what you are looking for.

Let's return to our atomic skill of *using movement to form a character.* Start by brainstorming some ideas. At this point, you don't need to edit yourself—just throw a bunch of ideas onto the page. How would you get students to practice moving in unusual ways that might inform a character choice? Jot down a few ideas and then turn the page.

Here's what my brainstorming came up with:

- Pretend you're a monster from a monster movie and move like that.
- Have someone whisper the name of an actor in your ear and walk like them.
- Toss Nerf® balls at each other and whatever body part gets hit with the ball is paralyzed and you move around like that.
- Picture your favorite cartoon character and walk like that.
- Pretend I have a dial and can make gravity go from 0– 100.
- Move like an animal.
- Walk like any animal that someone shouts out.
- Walk like an animal with an imaginary name that someone shouts out.
- Pick someone else in the room and move like them.
- Get a bunch of emotions and call them out and everyone embodies them.
- Move like you're old.
- Walk like you're a baby.
- Dance like a waif.
- Move like an oaf.
- Be a waifish oaf.
- Pretend you have a time machine and it can make you move like you're in any period in history.

Any of these ideas might get people to do interesting and specific movement on stage. I might select several of them to try over the course of the exercise.

What did you come up with? Did you have some fun ideas? Were some of them crazy? Were some of them variations on things you've seen before? That's okay! Let yourself be creative and then pick one (or more) that you want to develop further by thinking through the *mechanics* of the exercise—how will it work?

For example, let's say I want to try, "Pretend I have a dial and can make gravity go from 0–100." How will this exercise run? I could have students:

- Do this exercise while walking around the room.
- Up one at a time on stage while everyone watches.
- In groups of two or four.
- Spread around the room while everyone's back is turned so they don't feel self-conscious, then again when everyone's eyes are open.
- Visualize doing the exercise while seated first, then get up and perform in front of the class.

There's no right or wrong answer, as long as the students are learning, having fun, and feeling safe. My decision for how to run the exercise might be determined by where this exercise appears in the overall flow of the class (more on that in later chapters).

Part of the joy of teaching is the creativity you get to use in inventing new exercises and new ways to practice skills. Be creative!

Anticipate Different Physical Abilities

During your class planning, be sure you're not making assumptions about your students' abilities. You might come up with a fun character walk exercise, only to discover that one of your students is in a wheelchair and another one is on crutches with a broken foot. Have a backup plan in mind. For instance, a "walk" could be quickly modified to "physical movements and gestures." You could also have a backup exercise that builds character through something other than physical movement, like voice.

The time to consider gracefully accommodating all students is during your planning, not as you're scrambling to modify an exercise during class. More on accommodating students with disabilities in chapter 14.

Developing Exercises That Gradually Increase in Difficulty

Often, an exercise will have several "rounds," where you layer on new challenges one at a time. For example, in the last chapter, based on the class topic of creating stakes in our scenes, we identified "heightening" as an atomic skill. Here is one way to develop an exercise that starts out as easy as possible and then gradually becomes more challenging:

Skill to Learn: Heightening

Organize the students into two lines, so they can quickly take turns going up onto stage in pairs. Each student in the pair should come from one line (this is sometimes referred to as "layup lines" for fans of basketball). After everyone has had a turn from both lines, add a new challenge.

FIRST TIME THROUGH: One player enters and makes a mundane offer. The second player agrees and adds information to make the offer more important:

> Farouq: *"I picked some mushrooms."*
> Nicole: *"Those are poisonous mushrooms."*

SECOND TIME THROUGH: Players add a third line that heightens the scene further:

> Lizbet: *"This door is locked."*
> Shayne: *"I hear strange noises behind the door."*
> Lizbet: *"The noises started right after that meteorite fell to Earth."*

THIRD TIME THROUGH: Players continue heightening back and forth, until the scene can't heighten any further:

> Amitabh: *"I'm having oatmeal for breakfast."*
> Jin: *"It's your last meal."*
> Amitabh: *"I never expected to volunteer for this mission."*
> Jin: *"The fate of the planet is resting on you."*
> Amitabh: *"Tell our unborn daughter that I loved her."*

FINAL ROUND: Rather than building incrementally, players respond to the initial mundane offer with a fully heightened response:

> Pryce: *"I found a stick."*
> Kadyn: *"Finally, we can complete our raft and escape Monster Island!"*

If you had started this exercise by immediately challenging students to jump from a mundane offer to a fully heightened response, they would have struggled to make that leap. But by gradually adding steps each round, they develop the skill bit by bit.

Improv Exercises May Not *Look* Like Improv

Keep in mind that the individual exercises in your class do not need to look like improv. It's easy to imagine that atomic exercises in a scenework class need to look like scenes, or that atomic exercises in a music class need to look like music, but often, learning an atomic skill will not look like improv at all.

For example, imagine you're teaching a musical improv class about rhyme schemes: AABB or ABCB or ABAB. In the course of planning this class, you might realize that one atomic skill is simply "coming up with rhymes." After all, students can't execute a rhyme scheme in a song if they can't think of a word to rhyme. Thus, you might do an exercise where students simply stand around and practice coming up with rhymes for a given word—perhaps by cycling through the alphabet: "At, Bat, Cat, Fat, Gat, Hat, Lat, Mat," etc.

Does standing around and speaking rhymes look like improv? Nope. Does it look like a musical improv performance? Definitely not. And that's okay!

Another example might be convincing beginner students that they don't have to be "creative" to improvise. You could lead an exercise where each person tells lies about their life, proving that even the most "uncreative" student can easily improvise material. Standing in a circle and telling lies looks nothing like improv, but it's a remarkably effective way to show students that we all have the power to make stuff up!

Atomic skills are the building blocks that students use to create improv. As you figure out ways to teach your students new skills, absolutely anything is available to you—not just the recognizable "improv exercises."

To Invent or Borrow?

As you start developing your classes, you'll likely mix and match between exercises you've learned before and new exercises you've developed yourself. You may hear about an exercise from another teacher but want to put your own spin on it. Or you may have an idea for an exercise and want to try a couple of different approaches to see which works best. Have a plan, be ready to pivot off of things that don't work, and don't be afraid to experiment.

> *I really loved a recent class with Drew Bekas and Zach Mouriz where they let us do a whole exercise of "bad improv"—layups where we intentionally tried to break every rule in the book. Bad blocking, teaching scenes, transactions, negating each other. It solidified how far we've come and was cathartic to just get the rule breaking out of our system.*
>
> — Shannon O'Brien

How Hard Should Exercises Be?

Ideally, they should be just hard enough that students have to work to be successful. If everyone in the class can successfully complete an exercise on the first try, it's probably not hard enough. Learning happens just past the edge of competency. However, if *nobody* can successfully complete an exercise, it's likely too hard. You need to break it down further into smaller, more achievable atomic skills or beats.

Finding that sweet spot—where people are pushing themselves, maybe getting it wrong the first time, then getting it right with practice—that's where true learning happens.

For brand-new students, exercises should be easier and more achievable than those designed for more experienced improvisers. A new student isn't just learning to improvise—they're also gaining confidence with being up on stage in front of their peers. They need a lot of wins and a lot of positive feedback. In a beginners' class, an exercise where everybody finds instant success can be a great way to get started.

As students gain experience, you'll need to push them progressively harder, so they are challenged. Sometimes this means making exercises more difficult. Sometimes it means stacking skills atop one another so that a student has to keep track of multiple skills at the same time. A student may be able to perform bold characters in an individual exercise, but then subsequently drop their character work when they try to apply that to a scene. If that's the case, make sure your students aren't just doing character exercises and are also being challenged to apply what they've learned. (More about applying skills in the coming chapters.)

 When I first started teaching, I had an entire class walk out shaking their heads and looking sad. I knew I'd failed them. Too much "work" and not enough wins.

— Hadas Cassorla

Chapter 6
Overcoming Mental Blockers

When you think about it, teaching improv is weird.

After all, everyone already knows how to improvise. We literally improvise every minute of our lives. There is no script for when we walk into a bank to cash a check or sit down in a restaurant to order dinner. We improvise effortlessly as we go about our days.

And yet, as soon as a student gets up on stage, they suddenly lose the ability to listen and react honestly. Their brain goes into overdrive trying to figure out the "right" thing to say and do. The more we load students up with rules—"Don't ask questions" and "Make a character choice" and "Set the location"—the more we activate students' internal editors and bring all of their fears to the surface.

Yes, fears. Humans evolved to survive in close-knit social groups. You wouldn't last three days as a prehistoric cave-dweller without the rest of your tribe to help feed you, keep you warm, and protect you from marauding predators. Anthropologists and psychologists have documented that from an evolutionary standpoint, fitting in with the group is—for our primitive human brains—*literally* a matter of life and death.

That's why many people have a fear of public speaking (and improv). Even though there is no actual danger if you bomb on stage, your prehistoric brain still says, "Don't mess this one up! You might get ostracized and die a horrible death outside the cave."

It all adds up to students coming into class with a heap of fears, hesitancies, negative self-talk, and nervousness. Some show it on the outside, while others try to hide it and put on a brave face. As their teacher, you must help them navigate this hesitation. Your job goes beyond just teaching new skills. You also have to anticipate the negative beliefs and fears that prevent students from being successful and come up with mitigation strategies.

I call this "blocker removal."

What is a "Blocker?"

A mental "blocker" is any belief that prevents a student from being successful in your class. Often it takes the form of negative self-talk (either spoken or unspoken) about their ability to do something or learn something. Do any of these sound familiar?

"I could never do improv. I'm not quick enough."

"I'm not good at playing big characters because I'm shy."

"I can't play rap games. I don't have any sense of rhythm."

"I just don't have an ear for accents."

"I can't sing. I have a terrible voice."

"I'm afraid to edit. I don't want to ruin someone else's scene."

Belief in negative statements like these is a powerful thing. If your students believe they can't, they probably won't—and they may not even try. It's your job to help them believe that they can.

As you're planning your class, you need to play pop psychologist to anticipate blockers and how you'll remove them. Until you can help your students unshackle themselves from their negative self-talk, all of your carefully crafted skills and exercises will fall short.

How Do You Identify Blockers?

To accurately identify and mitigate blockers in your students, you'll need to use a combination of:

- **Your own experiences.** Can you remember your own fears and negative self-talk from when you were first learning improv skills? Do you still have fears and hesitancies that hold you back? (Most likely, the answer is yes!)

- **What you've seen and heard in other classes.** You've probably heard people say the things they *can't do* or *won't do* or *shouldn't do* (because they'll "ruin" the game or the show). Also keep an ear open for things students say they "hate." That's often a marker of fear.

- **A heaping scoop of empathy.** Put yourself in the shoes of someone learning your topic and imagine what it's like to not yet be good at it. Can you imagine the kinds of fears or beliefs that would prevent them from success? What might their own negative self-talk sound like?

Keep these thoughts in mind as you work with your students. You can also tap more seasoned teachers and ask them what kind of blockers they've seen in their classes.

Strategies for Removing Blockers

Removing blockers is absolutely critical. To succeed in improv, one has to make mistakes. Students who are racked with fears or negative self-talk won't push themselves past their comfort zone to where the learning happens. And worse yet, those "mistakes" will just reinforce the already negative feelings about their abilities.

There are three different strategies you can employ for removing blockers:

1. **Exercises** to help students achieve something they thought they couldn't.
2. **Reframing** blockers to show students why their blockers aren't real.
3. **Removing** blockers entirely by dismissing them as requirements.

Let's look at how this works. In the below example, imagine you are teaching a musical chorusing class and you've identified several blockers in your students.

Blocker: Fearing they will ruin the game if they don't follow the "right" song structure

Strategy: Exercise

For this blocker, you can develop an exercise to show them that their fear is unfounded. After getting this hesitant student up on stage with some of the class's more experienced singers, ask them to *purposefully* try to break the exercise. For instance, if the goal is to sing two lines and a chorus, have them sing three lines and a chorus—or any other incorrect formula. The job of the more experienced singers is to make it work.

Improv is remarkably forgiving. All the rules and structures we put on ourselves can be easily broken, rearranged, detached, fixed, and re-straightened. Your goal with this exercise is to show the student that "mistakes" in musical improv are no different than "mistakes" in any other scene. Improvisers will accept them, incorporate them, and make them work. Who cares if you sing three lines and then a chorus, or one line and then a chorus, or nothing but a chorus? When a group is working together and committing to the song, it will all work out (and the audience probably won't even notice).

This exercise shows the fearful student that breaking the intended structure won't break the game. In fact, when a song structure unexpectedly changes, it can be a great opportunity to discover something new.

Blocker: Believing they can't or shouldn't sing because they don't have a good voice

Strategy: Reframing

With this blocker, the student believes that their voice quality is the most important component of musical improv performance, but (as most experienced improvisers know) what the audience really cares about is *commitment.* We've all seen terrible singers who crush musical improv games through sheer character, energy, and enthusiasm. And we've all seen a bad singer kill it at karaoke by doubling down on commitment to the song.

For this reframing strategy, you might have the student get up and sing a song where their only goal is to sing loudly and with huge stage presence. Remind them that it's their *character* who is singing, not themselves. So, even if they feel that they personally do not have a good voice, they can win over the audience by choosing a character who sings loudly and fearlessly.

In my improv troupe, we have a saying: "If you can't sing, sing louder."

Blocker: Believing that they can't play musical games because they are bad at coming up with rhymes

Strategy: Removing

For this blocker, the best strategy is to simply *remove* it. Many students mistakenly believe that rhyming is necessary in musical improv, but unless it's a rhyming-elimination game (like "Da Doo Ron Ron"), rhyming is definitely *not* a requirement. Tell this student that nothing has to rhyme in their songs, and to prove it, have them get up and sing a few couplets without rhymes. You could also give examples of popular songs that have few or no rhymes (see Morissette, Alanis). Urge them to focus on commitment and emotion in their songs. It is possible to sing a perfectly great improv song with no rhymes.

This doesn't mean they shouldn't rhyme if they happen to do so, or that other students in the class shouldn't rhyme. It is simply removing the blocker by telling them that rhyming is 100 percent optional, and much less important than commitment to the song.

Many blockers can be removed by simply reframing or removing the fear through something you say. It's amazing how many students have talked themselves into believing they *can't* do something or *must* do something for the good of the format. Your job is to help them see that this belief is unnecessarily holding them back. By letting go of can't ... don't ... shouldn't ... won't they are ready to make new breakthroughs.

> ***"I could never do improv. I'm not quick enough."***
> —No problem, dramatic pauses captivate the audience.

> ***"I'm not good at playing big characters because I'm shy."***
> —Some of the best characters are created through point of view instead of big physical or vocal characteristics.

> ***"I can't play rap games. I don't have any sense of rhythm."***
> —Rap is a character game. Just be a huge character.

> ***"I'm afraid to edit. I don't want to ruin someone else's scene."***
> —Editing is a gift to help move the show along. If you

edit too soon, we can always bring the scene back for another beat.

Anticipating Blockers in Your Class

If you suspect that a particular blocker is widespread—for instance, students believing that they have to be "quick" or "clever" in order to succeed—you may want to make that blocker removal strategy a part of your syllabus. Your curriculum can mix blocker removers with skill development exercises.

On the other hand, if you think a blocker is less prevalent, you can simply keep the blocker removal strategy in your pocket, ready to throw into the mix if you see it affecting one or more students. Either way, anticipating blockers and coming up with exercises, reframes, or removals is critical to ensuring that your class is effective for all students.

 I was a very introverted improv student at first but saw amazing improvisers and wanted to be able to be free like them ... so when my teacher said "Mistakes are gold" it reminded me we are making it up ... have fun and don't worry about the outcome!!! Now I say it all the time to my students.

— Christina Cataldo

Chapter 7
Finalizing Your Syllabus

Your class is coming together! You've identified the key skills, exercises, blockers, and blocker removals. But there are a few more sections to plan before you'll be ready to write out and finalize your syllabus.

Plan to Put Skills Into Action

Improv skills don't exist in the abstract. We learn and improve skills so that we can get better at playing a game, performing a format, or putting on a show. In most cases, you'll want to finish your class by letting students take their newfound skills and apply them to a game or format.

For example, if your class topic is "creating more specific characters," you'll want to let students put their new skills into action by playing short-form games or performing scenes where they can flex their character muscles. Likewise, if your class topic is "leaning into authentic emotions," you will want to end with games, scenes, or a format that lets students practice emotional content.

Performing a skill during an exercise that is focused *specifically on that skill* is different from performing the skill in another game or format, where extra rules or requirements must be considered. You want to finish your classes with a real-world application of the skill students have just learned.

How long you spend on this is up to you and depends on the length of the class and how much time was needed to cover all the atomic skill exercises. I recommend reserving at least fifteen to twenty minutes toward the end of the session for applying skills.

Note: Not every class will require this. For instance, if your class is already focused on learning specific types of games (for example, rap games or naive character games) you may have already played the games over the course of the class and no further application is necessary.

Planning Warm-Ups

Even though warm-ups come first during class time, they are often the very last part of my syllabus that I plan. Warm-ups should be designed to complement the rest of your syllabus. Until you know exactly what you're teaching, it's hard to know how to plan a warm-up.

The most important aspect of designing warm-ups is to choose something that will actually warm people up, physically and mentally. Make sure you're choosing a warm-up game where everyone actively participates at once. Warm-ups where you "go around the circle" are often a poor choice, because students spend most of the time standing around and waiting. Instead, break the class into smaller circles or choose a warm-up that encourages simultaneous group participation.

TIP: MANY TEACHERS DO TOO MANY WARM-UPS AND WASTE VALUABLE CLASS TIME.

Plan one or two quick, high-energy warm-ups to get students into the right headspace, and then move on to your class exercises.

Warm-ups can (but do not have to) match the class topic. If you're teaching a character class, your warm-ups might incorporate elements that will complement your atomic skills, such as a character walk or "Zip Zap Zop" in character voices. On the other hand, it's absolutely fine for a warm-up to simply get people moving, laughing, and connecting—even if it has no real relation to your class topic. Energy and full group participation are much more important than matching the class topic.

Finally: for heaven's sakes, have your warm-ups planned. Don't try to wing it, and don't show up and say, "Who has a favorite warm-up?" Not having warm-ups prepared signals to the class that you aren't prepared to teach and diminishes your authority. Always come in with one or two brief, energetic, and focused warm-ups ready to go.

Planning the Right Amount of Material and Time

It can be hard to know how much to plan for a class. Plan too much material and you risk running out of time before you've effectively stacked your atomic skills or having to rush through your syllabus. Plan too little material and you risk running out of activities before the end of class.

In my experience, it's best to plan a *little* too much. During the class, you may realize that the students are learning faster than you anticipated, and you can skip certain exercises. Or you may start an exercise only to realize that it's not really working, and you need to adjust. I like to have enough material on my syllabus that I can switch to a different option when something isn't working well or when the students are hungry to learn faster.

Try to come up with several possible exercises for each atomic skill and choose just one during the class. When planning for the last portion of class, jot down a list of five possible games, knowing there may only be time to play one or two. Remember: these options are so *you* have flexibility; you shouldn't share them with the class or ask them to choose which they prefer—be decisive and be in control.

How to Estimate the Time Needed for Exercises

How long any single exercise takes will depend on the length of the exercise, how many times you repeat it, whether everyone in class participates, etc. While building your syllabus, you should have a *rough* idea of how much time you'll need. Let's look at an example of how you might estimate this.

Imagine that you have twenty students. You'd like all of them to participate in an exercise where they perform one-minute scenes in pairs. As a baseline, this means you'll be doing ten different one-minute scenes, for a total of ten minutes. But that doesn't mean the full exercise is only going to take ten minutes—you also have to factor in the following:

- How long it takes to explain or set up the exercise.
- Transition time between each pair of students.
- Reflection/discussion time after each pair has gone.
- Reflection/discussion time after the exercise has ended.

Let's estimate that it will take you one minute to explain the exercise (hopefully no longer than this, if you've kept your atomic skill small). And let's say that after each pair performs, you give a few quick notes of praise before bringing the next two students up onto stage—budgeting about one minute for this discussion and transition time. After everyone has performed, you'll spend another minute asking students to reflect on what they discovered.

Based on those variables (math!), we've added another ten minutes of reflection/transition time (one minute after each pair), plus one minute of discussion at the end. We're now at twenty-one total minutes for the entire exercise. All of this assumes that the one-minute scenes don't run long, that you keep reflections and transitions efficient, and that discussion after the exercise has ended is concise. Just to be safe, we might allot twenty-five minutes for the entire exercise. That's a good chunk of the class!

In a later chapter, we'll talk more about how to control the flow of a class by adjusting things like exercise length, the number of students who participate in each exercise, and discussion/transition time. If you have several skills you want to cover, you'll need to be efficient with the timing.

A good rule of thumb: *everything* always takes longer than you think it will.

Include Estimated Timing on Your Syllabus

I highly recommend putting actual timing of exercises on your syllabus. Consider blocking your class into fifteen-minute increments, and be ready to move on when it's time for the next exercise. Or, if your exercises don't fit into neat fifteen-minute blocks, write out the specific timing you intend to follow. It's very easy to let time get away from you in a class! Write out the actual clock times, so you're not doing math during the class (i.e. "Exercise 2 starts at 8:05 p.m."). You can see what this looks like by reviewing the sample syllabus at the companion site.

> *I was at a class at a festival where the teacher never got past the warm-ups.*
>
> — Teylor Burke

What Happens If You Go Through Your Syllabus Faster than Planned?

If you get through all of your planned exercises sooner than expected, don't panic! Because your syllabus has left time at the end for putting new skills into action, you can easily adjust by having more play time. If your final planned exercise ends with thirty minutes left in the class, that gives you thirty minutes to play games or perform a format that apply those skills.

And of course, *never* tell students that you've run out of material! There's nothing more demoralizing than a teacher saying, "Well, that's all I had planned, I guess we're done." As a teacher, you always have more to give and you should transition seamlessly into applying the class skill with games, scenes, or a format until the end.

Allow for Extra Time to Wrap Up the Class

Make sure to plan time for wrap-up and reflection at the end of your class. If your class is scheduled to end at 9 p.m., that doesn't mean you should run exercises right up until 9 p.m.

You'll need to start wrapping up at least ten minutes early to allow time for questions, reflections, housekeeping, and appreciation.

It can be tempting to throw in *just one more exercise* before wrapping up, but give yourself those ten minutes at the end to calmly and gracefully end the class while letting students out on time. You'll be glad you did.

And that's your class plan! You've got your topic. You've broken the topic down into atomic skills and developed exercises. You've identified blockers and come up with games or a format to let the students apply their learnings at the end of class. You've planned your warm-ups.

And you've scheduled in enough time at the end for wrap-up and reflection.

Congratulations, you've built a solid syllabus for your first class and you're ready to meet your students. In the next section, we'll get into the classroom and start teaching.

Chapter 8
It's Class Day!

I t's time for class!

Maybe you're teaching a group of new students that you've never met before, stepping in to teach the weekly drop-in at your theater, or perhaps leading your own troupe's weekly rehearsal. Whatever the class, let's get set up for success.

Arrive Early

As the teacher, you want to be one of the first people to arrive —*the* first if you can. I like to arrive at least thirty minutes before the class starts, allowing plenty of time for unexpected traffic, parking difficulties, finding the classroom (if it's not at your regular theater), and any other potential hiccups. The last thing you want to do is roll into the classroom stressed out about being late or out of breath from sprinting across a parking lot.

If you're in an unfamiliar space, you can use this time to make sure you have enough chairs (if needed), know how to operate any required lights or audio equipment, and know where the bathrooms are. Walk around just to make sure the space is comfortably set up and appropriate for your class. I have shown up to teach at spaces where:

- The doors were locked.
- Nobody knew how to turn on the lights.
- The bathrooms were out of order.
- There was garbage strewn about from a previous class.
- The chairs were all stacked in another room.
- The audio-visual equipment couldn't be turned on (for a class where I needed A/V).
- The audio couldn't be turned *off* and I was in danger of having to compete with the soulful sounds of Peaches & Herb.
- It was 85 degrees in the theater and nobody knew how to operate the air conditioning.

As the teacher, any problems you encounter are *your* problems, so you're going to want to show up early enough to solve them.

Greet Students as They Arrive

By getting to class early, you also have the advantage of greeting each student as they arrive. Don't stand in a corner talking with your friends—make it a point to welcome every-body as they come into the room. Tell them your name, that you're their teacher for the session, and start building rapport. Students may also want to share something with you before class—a question, a concern, or a limitation. Being available as they enter the room makes it safe and easy for them to do so. Some of my students have shared things with me upon arrival like:

"I have to leave a half hour early to pick up my husband from the airport."

"I'm deaf in one ear so please speak loudly when addressing me and don't be offended if I ask you to repeat yourself."

"My uncle died this morning and I'm in a bad headspace, but I didn't want to be alone. Can I attend but not get up on stage today?"

"I have arthritis in my knees and can only stand for a few minutes at a time."

Knowing any physical, emotional, and time limitations will help you make sure that every student is properly accommodated. You'll avoid uncomfortable and awkward situations during class.

Remember, You're "On Stage"

As an improv student, you're probably used to chatting with friends, goofing off, checking your phone, or eating a snack until the teacher calls the class to order. But as the teacher, don't forget that you're "on" from the moment you walk into the room until the moment the last student leaves at the end of class. You don't have the luxury of waiting to turn on your "teaching persona" at the last minute.

As soon as you enter the room, have your teacher hat on and show your friendly, confident, energetic, positive self. And if you're tired, stressed, or have had a rough day? TOUGH. As the teacher, you are required to radiate excitement from the moment you arrive. If students sense that you don't fully want to be there, they won't fully want to be there, either.

If you're an introvert, this may mean pushing yourself out of your comfort zone. Greeting new people and confidently talking to strangers may not be something you are naturally comfortable with. You can think of the situation as requiring you to *play the role of teacher*. As soon as you step into the class-room, you're "on stage" and playing that part.

> TIP: DRESS FOR SUCCESS! YOU DON'T HAVE TO WEAR A BALL GOWN, BUT MAYBE LEAVE THE PIZZA-STAINED T-SHIRT IN THE LAUNDRY HAMPER. SHOW THAT YOU MADE AN EFFORT.

Bring Your Written Syllabus

Along with arriving early, always bring a written syllabus for your class. You should not have to (and should not try to) memorize your syllabus. Write or type it out on paper and bring it with you. Ideally, bring a printed copy *and* a digital backup on your phone. More times than I care to admit, I have accidentally left my printed syllabus at home or reached the theater only to discover that I have no connectivity on my phone. Do yourself a favor and make sure you arrive prepared.

Additionally, bringing a written syllabus to class communi-cates to your students that you are organized and have a plan. You should never feel shy about referring to your syllabus. You do not need to be "off book" to teach effectively.

One more thing: if you're viewing the syllabus on your phone, be sure to tell your students that's what you're doing. It can be disconcerting to see the teacher constantly checking their phone and seeming distracted.

Develop Your Teaching Persona

In the first section of this book, we talked about all the attributes that define a great improv teacher: positive, energetic, empathetic, inspirational, and so on. If you're not naturally the most energetic or positive person, you'll need to leverage some of your own improv skills to wear those hats while you teach. Remember, you're playing a part.

While your teaching persona should be authentically *you*, it should also be a heightened version of yourself that assures students they're in good hands. These are the most important attributes to showcase in your teaching persona:

Confidence

Improv can be scary and emotional for students. You're asking them to stand up in front of their peers and take risks, play crazy characters, explore real emotions, or even reveal their truest selves. Students need to feel confident in your ability to guide them on this journey. The more confidence you portray as the teacher, the more confidence they will feel and the more they will buy into the class.

Students should trust that you've got their back and that they will be safe and supported. They also need to believe that you have a plan and that you will effectively help them learn.

Part of portraying confidence is making executive decisions and showing strong leadership. Avoid saying things like: "Would you like to keep doing this exercise or move on?" or "Do you want to work on scene starts or edits today?"—which can come across as lacking confidence and planning. Strive to make strong, confident decisions rather than politely trying to offer options. You're the leader, not a server at Applebee's.

If you're a brand-new teacher, it's likely you'll feel anything but confident. This is your "fake it 'til you make it" moment. Act like you got this, even if you are trembling on the inside.

Positivity

You can never be too positive as an improv teacher. Small wins should be celebrated as huge victories, and mistakes should be celebrated as positive learning opportunities. Greet students as they enter the room with enthusiasm and excitement. Introduce the class and tell them it's going to be a great night. Lead applause after each exercise and praise the little things. You want your students to truly believe that everything done during the class is worth celebrating. After all, getting up on stage in front of people without a script is pretty audacious. Make sure it's fun, too!

Energy

Your teaching energy will drive the entire class's energy. If you are upbeat, the students will respond in kind. If you are dragging, the students will drag, too.

I once attended a truly terrible "master class" at an improv festival, where the (very famous) teacher stumbled in one minute before class time clutching a cup of coffee, wearily dropped into a chair with a groan, and proceeded to "direct" us while barely moving (except to take a smoke break). Yuck.

As a teacher, you don't have the luxury of wearing your bad day on your sleeve. Your energy will set the tone in your classroom either for success or for mediocrity.

My goal as a teacher is to never sit down during the class. I know that if I sit down, my energy and alertness will drop. Is it tiring? Yep. Does it keep me focused and energetic for the entire class? Also yep. (If you have physical limitations that prevent you from standing for the entire class, please know that I am not judging you. This is my personal goal, not yours.)

Fun fact: the activity tracker device that I wear on my wrist says I burn more calories teaching an improv class than I do running a 5K race—and I believe it!

No Apologies

Even if you're teaching your first class *ever*, you shouldn't admit that to the class or apologize for your lack of experience. You may be incredibly nervous inside, but outwardly, it's vital to project a sense of confidence, competency, and authority. No matter how tempting it is to admit that you don't have much teaching experience or to beg students to go easy on you, it will only make teaching more difficult if the students are nervous about your qualifications.

If you've been tapped to teach the class, then *you're the teacher*, and you should hold your head up proudly as you lead the session.

Chapter 9
Winning the Beginning: How to Start Your Class

At the start of class, your students are likely nervous, excited, curious about you as a teacher, and wondering what to expect. In just the first few minutes, you need to win their attention and promote confidence in your ability to lead. Starting your class in an assured, organized manner gets the students on your side and helps make a positive first impression.

Start on Time

Unless there's a compelling reason not to start on time (overturned busload of nuns blocking the freeway, classroom was changed to a new location at the last minute, etc.), endeavor to begin your class promptly. You don't want to cheat the students who have showed up on time and you don't want to reinforce the idea that you'll wait for latecomers. Your theater may have a different standard, but it's typically best to start promptly. Build your reputation as a teacher who respects students' time.

If you are intentionally beginning late, announce at the official starting time that you are doing so and why. For example: "We'll be starting five minutes late today because of the parking lot being closed" or "We'll start five minutes after the hour because that's the theater policy." Make sure students know that you're aware of the time and starting late on purpose.

When latecomers arrive, do not make an effort to catch them up on what they missed. Don't re-explain the warm-up or exercise in progress. And don't reiterate anything you already said at the beginning of class. If they can't seamlessly join the warm-up already in progress, let them know they can join the next one. If you accommodate their lateness, you will train the class that it's okay to be late and waste the time of those who were prompt.

Win the First Two Minutes

When it's class time, circle up the students and "win" those first two minutes. In other words, start the class with confidence, know exactly what you're going to say, and take full control. You may want to rehearse the first few minutes of your class beforehand, so you know exactly how it's going to flow. Students are ready to make a snap judgement based on how you conduct yourself; a strong, confident start immediately gets them on your side.

One way to do this is by waiting for class start time, proceeding to the center of the room, and *loudly* saying, "Let's circle up!" You're not asking—you're instructing. Be confident and in control.

Inevitably, stragglers will be slow to enter the circle, and some people may be wrapping up side conversations. Herd them into the circle and make sure you have everyone's focus as you begin. When you speak, do so loudly and confidently. Look around the circle and make eye contact. You want every student to believe that you are in total control and that they are in good, safe hands.

Introduce Yourself

The very first thing you should do once the students have circled up is introduce yourself. Tell them your name and any credentials *("I've been a member of Monkey Bunch Improv for three years")*. Don't worry if you think your experience isn't very impressive—it's okay to omit your credentials if you don't have any yet or feel unconfident in the ones you do have.

I often see teachers shoot themselves in the foot at this point by saying things like:

> *"Sorry, this is my first time teaching."*

> *"There are better teachers."*

> *"This is my first time teaching this."*

> *"I'm trying an experiment today."*

> *"I took this class at a festival and I'm going to try to do it justice."*

It's natural to be humble and want to lower expectations, but instead be confident and in control.

After introducing yourself, take a moment to express your excitement for the class and share any housekeeping items (you can make a list of housekeeping items at the beginning of your syllabus so you don't have to try to remember everything). I usually like to tell students that we'll be ending at the scheduled time, whether we take a break in the middle of the class or not, and that we'll leave time at the end for reflection and questions.

Introduce the Workshop

Next, you want to introduce the class itself and the skills you'll be workshopping. You can go into greater detail after the warm-ups, but it's critical to start by telling students exactly what the class is about. People are better learners when they are first primed for learning.

This is the perfect time to share your "I've noticed" statement and your class topic thesis, almost verbatim. Here's an example:

> *"I've noticed that we tend to have a lot of arguments and negotiations in our scenes. Because of that, we often get stuck and have trouble moving the story forward. Today we're going to work on techniques to avoid arguments and get past negotiations so we can do more dynamic scenes where the performers are on the same page and the story progresses."*

This level of explicit clarity about the problem, why the problem matters, and what success will look like gives students a mental framework for understanding the class.

Even if students were previously furnished with a class description, always share this detailed information right at the beginning—just assume nobody was paying attention when they signed up. I can't emphasize this enough: **explain your class thesis right at the beginning so students know what to expect.**

Set Boundaries, Establish Consent, and Discuss Content

Your next order of business is to talk about boundaries, consent, and class content. You should always go over this information right at the beginning of class. This is *especially* important for new students, students who are new to your theater, or any situation where people are working together for the first time. Your theater or festival may have its own standards and guidelines, and if so, you should adhere to those.

If you don't have set standards and guidelines to work from, here are some helpful boundaries to communicate:

No Touching

The standard for new students should simply be "no touching other people." Period. It is not helpful to ask students about their individual boundaries or personal comfort level with being touched, because new students may not even understand what that means in an improv context. Students also may not feel comfortable sharing their limitations and will likely not remember each other's requests. It's best to prohibit touching altogether.

Avoid Uncomfortable Content

Content that is sexual, violent, or emotionally disturbing in nature is unwelcome. Students should not harass other students by putting them in situations or bringing up subject matter that could be uncomfortable or triggering. Students are there to have fun, not to be edgy or to test each other's boundaries.

Any Student Can Stop an Exercise at Any Time

Improv involves playing pretend in the class, but students always have the power to stop an exercise. If anything in an exercise causes a student to feel discomfort, they may—with no judgement—stop immediately. You may also add that it is *your* job as the teacher to stop scenes if you suspect discomfort. This adds to your authority and can help people feel safe.

Here's a sample script for how to deliver these rules to your students:

"When an improv troupe has been working together for a long time, they set their own guidelines for how they interact and the content they are comfortable with. Because we're new to each other, in this class we're going to default to very distinct boundaries so nobody is made uncomfortable.

One limitation is our physical bodies. Different people have different levels of comfort with being touched, so our rule is going to be simple: no touching each other in this class. Can we all agree to that? Good.

We're also going to avoid uncomfortable content or putting our classmates in uncomfortable situations. We're going to stay away from sex, violence, or emotionally disturbing scenarios. There's a whole world of fun we can play with, so we don't have to 'go there.'

And while one of the tenets of improv is saying 'Yes,' you are never obligated to say yes to anything that makes you uncomfortable in this class.

We'll all do our best to stay within the boundaries we've set, but if something crosses your own personal line you are always welcome to stop any exercise or scene and say, 'I'm uncomfortable with this,' and we'll respect that with no judgement."

You should develop your own version of this sample speech. The most important thing is to set very clear boundaries and uphold those boundaries during the course of the class. We'll talk more about what to do when boundaries get crossed in chapter 14.

What About Profanity?

In my classes, I set a rule that students may not use profanity. I find that students often use profanity to get a cheap laugh in lieu of making smart improv choices. Some students are also offended by off-color language.

You'll have to decide for yourself what kind of language you will allow in your class, but I feel that banning swear words leads to higher-quality work and helps train students to perform in a wider range of venues. I also personally outlaw scenes about bodily fluids—no poo-poo, pee-pee, vomit, or diarrhea. Nobody wants to watch that.

One way to clearly communicate these boundaries is by saying:

> *"In this class we're not going to use profanity or do scenes about bodily functions—pooping, barfing, etc. We're going to play at the top of our intelligence and do quality work, not bathroom humor."*

If something does come up during class—like a gratuitous F-bomb or random, mimed barfing—you can simply call out "New choice!" and have the student make a different offer while the exercise continues.

Learn the Names of Your Students

The next order of business is to learn your students' names—and this step is crucial. To effectively teach, you *must* be able to call on students by name. This applies to side coaching, calling specific people up onto the stage, or when giving notes and feedback.

Learning names also builds trust. Names are powerful! When you use somebody's name, you instantly create a bond and your coaching will be much better received.

Improv is also about group mind and ensemble. Making sure all the *students* know each other and feel a sense of kinship is part of your mission as the teacher. A class where everyone knows everyone else is much more fun than a class of strangers.

If you think that you're "bad with names," there's a quick and easy strategy to learn everybody's name right away. It is a visual mnemonic technique used by competitive memory champions. You *can* learn and remember everyone's name immediately. Here's how to do it:

The Visual Mnemonic Technique

While standing in the circle at the beginning of class, go around the circle and ask each person to share their name and why they're in the class (or why they first took improv, or what they're currently working on in their improv journey). The question is partly to get to know them and partly to give you an extra moment to memorize their name.

When the person says their name, create in your mind a visual reference to associate them with that name. Making it *visual* is extremely important. The visual cue will be what triggers your memory of their name.

Here are some examples:

> For **Mike**, you might picture him holding a microphone and doing stand-up comedy. In your mind's eye, visualize him up on stage, talking into the mic. Every time you look at him, you'll picture him holding the microphone, and your brain will go **microphone → mic → Mike!**

> For **Olivia**, you might picture her holding a martini glass and eating olives off a skewer. **Martini glass → eating olives → Olivia!**

> For **Jason**, you might think of the Jason character from the *Friday the 13th* movie and picture him with a hockey mask. **Hockey mask → Friday the 13th → Jason.**

For **Tai**, you might picture them wearing a tie-dye shirt. **Tie-dye** → **Tai.**

The more ridiculous, absurd, baroque, or wild your visual association, the easier it will be to remember. There is no right or wrong association. It's whatever you can quickly remember in your mind's eye.

The hardest names to remember are those from a country or culture different than your own. If you're an American teacher, finding a visual association for the name Przemysław may be tricky. If you only speak Cambodian, the name Heather might be tough. If you're struggling with a very unfamiliar name, ask the person to help teach it to you so you'll remember; it's likely they will have done that before.

If you are anxious about learning names, you can also write down names as students enter and you greet them. Use the few minutes before class to work on memorizing them, using visual association. Write unusual names phonetically if it helps.

Once everyone has said their name in the circle and you have (hopefully!) learned them, it's time to make sure that *everybody* learns them. To start, go around the circle again and point at each person and say their name. For each student, recall the visual association you made and (with luck) their name will pop into your head. If not, politely ask them to remind you.

Follow that up with a group "name game" of your choice. Pick one you've learned before or invent your own! The important thing is that everyone learns everyone's names and you can address each student correctly.

Clap It Up

As mentioned before, you cannot have too much positive energy at an improv class.

For this reason, any time you finish an exercise, I recommend saying, "Let's clap it up," and leading everyone in applause for the work done. This is a positive celebration that also signals a transition from one exercise into the next. Finished a warm-up? Clap it up! Finished an exercise? Clap it up! Just played a game? Clap it up!

Don't save the applause only for "successful" scenes or exercises. Get in the habit of clapping it up after everything, simply to say, "We are celebrating that we did this work together."

> *I remember a tennis coach I had once. He would always point out something positive and was very enthusiastic about it towards his students and then he'd follow it with a suggestion for improvement. So, being enthusiastic has been helpful for me as an educator and as a learner on the receiving end.*
>
> —Joseph W. Lemmo

Chapter 10
Keeping Things Moving: Mastering the Classroom

Now that you've won the first two minutes, introduced yourself, explained the class topic, set boundaries, and learned names, it's time to move on to your first warm-ups and exercises. This chapter will teach you how to keep your workshop flowing and seamlessly moving from segment to segment.

A class is no different than a movie, a book, or an improv show. It has a beginning, a middle, and an end. Each exercise is like a scene. How you order and transition between exercises is the key to making the experience effective and compelling. Move between exercises too quickly, and students won't have a chance to grasp each concept. Move too slowly, and people will get bored and the energy will drop. It's up to you to "read the room" and make transitions at the right time.

We've all been in improv classes that seemed to drag. Exercises went on long past the time that everyone "got it." Scenes that should have been cut off after a minute went on for five. Students started breaking into side conversations and fiddling with their phones. It's imperative that you manage the flow of the class so it's always moving forward at just the right pace.

Your syllabus is a roadmap, but once you're in the midst of the class, you must always be ready to adjust—by adding or removing and lengthening or shortening exercises—to keep the energy up and the students engaged.

Know When to Move On

Deciding when to transition from one exercise to the next is one of the most important decisions you'll make in class. Since your class is composed of atomic skills that build atop one another, it's important that students fully understand each exercise and concept before you move on to the next one. But because your time is limited, it's also important that you not run individual exercises for too long.

Imagine that you're teaching a class on "time jumps," where the goal is to edit one scene and then start a new, related scene that takes place at some point in the future. Your atomic skills might be:

Skill 1: Starting a scene

Skill 2: The mechanics of editing a scene (sweeps, edits, etc.)

Skill 3: Editing a scene once the *who* and the *where* have been established

Skill 4: Starting a new scene set in the future, connected to the first scene

What would happen if you moved on from skill 2 (the mechanics of editing a scene) before everyone had grasped that skill? It would be very hard to edit and start a connected scene if students didn't yet understand the mechanics of editing. And it would be hard for students to know when to edit if they didn't grasp waiting until the *who* and the *where* had been established. Skill 4 is directly dependent on the students understanding and being able to execute all skills 1–3. If you move on too quickly, it may not even be possible to successfully complete the objective of your class.

On the other hand, it's entirely possible that your class is very comfortable setting a who and a where, and are experienced with the mechanics of editing. In that case, after running a few rounds of skill 3, you may intuit as a teacher that they are ready to move on to skill 4. There's no reason to keep practicing something if the students have got it. Move on as soon as you sense that most of the class understands a skill.

Before Moving On, Should Everyone Do Each Exercise?

In a small class, it's possible that every student will get up to do every exercise. In larger classes, that's going to limit the number of exercises you can include and the speed with which you can get to your final objective.

If it seems like most of the students have mastered a skill, it's okay to move on to the next exercise. However, if it seems like only a few of the students are mastering a skill, it's better to stay on that exercise until a majority of folks have gotten it.

As the class progresses, you may also get a feel for which students have advanced skills and which ones need extra work. Often, the students who are best at an exercise will want to get up—because who doesn't want to shine in front of their peers? At the same time, the people who really need the practice often hang back because they don't want to "fail" in front of the class. In that case, you can decide who gets up for each exercise to ensure that the people who need the most practice get that opportunity before moving on.

It may feel more "fair" if everyone gets a go at an exercise, but there's a real danger that you'll blow through too much class time. Be intentional about which exercises everybody needs to do and which can be done by just some of the students.

And if the energy ever seems to be flagging, move on!

Stay Moving by Putting the Next Students "On Deck"

When you're moving through an exercise, consider having an "on deck" area where the students who are up next prepare to go. As soon as one group moves onto stage, other students jump up to fill in the "on deck area," ready to go.

Having a designated waiting area considerably shortens the turnaround time between groups. Instead of waiting for people to politely decide who goes next and make their way up to the stage, you always have the next group queued up and ready to go.

[Editor's note: "On deck" is either a nautical term or an American baseball term, depending on whether you're a Caribbean pirate or a Pittsburgh Pirate.]

Come Prepared with Suggestions or Assign Helpers

Another thing that burns valuable time in classes is coming up with suggestions for exercises. A class with lots of quick exercises can need dozens of "ask-fors" over the course of the session. Not only does getting these suggestions take time, but it can also mentally exhaust you, the teacher, by having to constantly ask for and choose suggestions.

Here are a few ways to make this quicker and easier:

- Come prepared with lists of suggestions. This is not a show. You're not trying to prove to the audience that everything is spontaneous. There's absolutely nothing wrong with bringing a printout of the exact type of suggestions you'll need for each exercise. (Hint: ChatGPT or your favorite AI can make quick work of this.)

- Designate one or more students as suggestion-gatherers. Tell them what kind of suggestions you'll need for an exercise and put them in charge of gathering those from the students and calling out which one is next. (You can always veto a suggestion if it doesn't work for the exercise.)

- Use the Sokkyo app for iOS or Android.

One caution: students in class often want to give "clever" suggestions to show how funny they can be, and those may not be the best choices to help the students on stage succeed. For example, if you're doing a spacework class where students are identifying and using objects in their location, the clever suggestion that an object is "inside a dog" may be hilarious (and a wonderful idea to explore in a show), but not the best way to help your students master the skill in practice.

Ensure Equal Participation

Part of your job as the teacher is to ensure roughly equal stage time for everyone. Left to their own devices, students will often self-select into the following categories:

- Shy or scared students who rarely (or never) get up on stage
- "Fairness-minded" students who get up once everyone else has had a chance to go
- "Stage hogs" who get up repeatedly
- "Couples" of students who only get up in pairs with their favorite classmates
- And opportunistic students who only get up with those they think are "good" to perform with

You should nip these self-selections in the bud. Everyone should learn to play with everyone else—skilled or beginner. If you simply say, "Three people on stage," you will inevitably see the stage hogs rush forward and the scared students hang back. You want to be proactive.

There are a couple of methods you can use to ensure equal stage time and a mix of who plays with whom. The simplest method is to draw names from a hat. Before class, write each student's name on a piece of paper (bonus: it helps you to learn names!) and draw for who will participate in each exercise. Once everyone has gone, return the papers to the hat and start again. This works well for exercises where you expect everyone to get up.

A second method is for *you* to choose who gets up for each exercise. This is a little trickier (because you must keep track of who has already gone and who hasn't), but it allows you to ensure specific students try the exercises they need the most.

Most students actually prefer having the teacher decide who gets up for each exercise. It takes all the pressure off, because they don't have to be "brave" about deciding to go. And even students who spend most of the class angling to play with their friends or favorites ultimately enjoy not having to constantly try to get up at just the right time with the right people.

Constantly monitor the group to make sure there aren't shy students who are trying to skip exercises. Often, they will be hiding in the back of the room, furiously avoiding eye contact with you. These are the students who need your heartiest encouragement!

> *Once I volunteered for the first exercise of the first class. During the second exercise, I didn't even raise my hand. Later the trainer asked everyone who didn't volunteer for the second exercise to share why. I said, "Well, I had already volunteered once. I wanted to give room for others."*
>
> *And she asked me, "But did you want to volunteer?" I nodded. Then she explained that this is one of our inner traps—we want to be nice and kind, and helpful, so we don't follow our inner drive. However, we can actually give others more when we are simply ourselves. This will help your team more than holding your natural self-expression in.*
>
> — Elina Biseniece

Encouraging Scared or Shy Students

Many of your students are probably scared. Newer students are far from their comfort zone, and even experienced improvisers are afraid of looking bad in front of their peers. Scared students will have plenty of excuses for why they're not getting up on stage, some of which they'll tell you, and some of which they're telling themselves internally:

"I learn better by watching."

"I don't want to ruin the exercise for everyone else."

"I need to see it a few times before I get up to try it."

"I'm going to fail."

"I'm bad at this, so there's no point practicing it."

"I get it, so there's no reason to do it."

Students need to get up and do the things they fear. "Go when you're most afraid" is a good reminder. You can do your students a favor and just tell them when it's their turn to get up on stage, eliminating their internal bargaining. Psychologically, it's a lot more comfortable to get up when the teacher makes you do it than when you have to make the choice yourself.

Mix It Up, So Everyone Plays with Everyone

If your best students only play with your best students and your least experienced students only play with your least experienced students, everybody loses. A more experienced student can help a less experienced person succeed in an exercise by virtue of their stronger skill set. At the same time, the more experienced student will build stronger skills because they'll have to do more listening and supporting. I always judge the skill of an improviser not by how well they can perform with other skilled improvisers, but by how well they can perform with less-skilled improvisers. These uneven pairings benefit everyone.

Similarly, watch out for "couples" who only want to play together or opportunists who only jump up for exercises with specific people. In a robust class, everyone plays with everyone.

Talk Less (Way Less)

You have to talk to teach. You have to introduce the class topic, describe formats, explain why a skill is important, side coach, and give feedback. But many teachers treat class like a lecture, going on at length about improv theory, sharing anecdotes, and waxing poetic about philosophy. Unless you are teaching an *actual* theory class, you should be as concise as possible to maximize student stage time for learning and practice.

Some specific areas to avoid spending too much time talking:

Explaining formats, games, or techniques instead of demonstrating

If you're trying to teach a complicated format (a Harold, for instance) you'll only confuse students with a ten-minute lecture on how the format works. Instead, break the Harold into individual atomic skills and exercises and build understanding piece by piece. If it takes you more than thirty seconds to explain how something works, chances are the students will struggle to follow along. When teaching a short-form game, explain the minimum before students get up to try, rather than giving them all the bullet points, gimmicks, variations, and keys to success ahead of time. Be especially careful not to share long lists of "things I've seen people do in this game that were very funny." Let the students discover!

Lengthy monologues on improv theory, history, or philosophy

A small amount of theory is good. Knowing the *why* behind any skill or exercise is critical to helping students learn. But nobody needs a fifteen-minute speech on the importance of establishing the location of the scene. It can be intoxicating to have the attention of twenty students and a platform to share your most cherished improv philosophies, but maybe write a blog post (or—*wink, wink*—a book) and save class time for practice!

Extended discussions after every exercise

Some analysis may be helpful after an exercise to eval-uate why it did or didn't work and to praise elements that were successful. But if you find yourself engaging in lengthy reviews of two-minute scenes, it probably means you aren't side coaching enough in the moment.

Besides striving to talk less and create more stage time, you may also need to limit comments and discussion from your students. This becomes a greater challenge as you get into more advanced classes (especially if you have—*ahem*—other improv teachers taking your class who have their own theo-ries, anecdotes, and philosophies more than ready to share).

It's easy for a class to dissolve into a free-for-all where every exercise ends with students talking about how *they* would have done it. Avoid burning time by allowing students to over-discuss what they think worked and didn't work, tales from past shows, opinions on how improv should be played, and so on. A dose of enthusiasm from the class is wonderful, but it's up to you to manage class time so the focus remains on doing exercises, not swapping stories.

It is not necessary—and often a big time suck—to follow each exercise by asking if anyone in the room has any comments. As the teacher, most of the feedback should be from *you*—and most of it should be in the form of side coaching during the exercise, not in extended analysis afterward.

Watch for Energy Drops

As class progresses, monitor the energy in the room to ensure that people aren't flagging. Once students get bored, tired, or fidgety, it's hard to regain their interest and enthusiasm. Energy drops not only affect the focus of the students who are on stage doing exercises, but also robs them of an engaged audience.

Here are some ways to keep the energy up in your class:

Vary the types of exercises and the number of students on stage. If you've just done a series of two-person exercises, consider following that with a six-person exercise or layup lines to get people out of their seats and moving around. You can plan for this while putting together your class syllabus, but also be prepared to switch things up on the fly if you notice the energy waning.

Limit the length of individual exercises. If students

do three-minute scenes instead of six-minute scenes, you'll cycle through twice as many exercises during the course of the class. Sometimes the length of an exercise is unavoidable—for instance, if the whole point of the class is to help students sustain longer scenes, it does no good to cut down the time—but often teachers let exercises go on *way* too long. Don't wait for students to make the right choices, but gently steer them in the proper direction with side coaching.

Talk less. We've covered this. If you've been talking for more than a minute, be aware that people are probably tuning you out.

If all else fails, stop the class and do an energy booster. There's nothing wrong with just tossing a high-energy, group warm-up game into the middle of your class when everyone has been sitting for a long time. Sometimes you just need a quick energy boost!

Another sign that the energy and focus is waning is when students break into side conversations. This often happens between exercises, when the teacher is engaged in setup or transitioning students on and off the stage. Be aware of side conversations and work to bring the focus back to the stage and to yourself, being commanding if needed. Once your class gets bored or distracted, it's hard to get them back. Keeping students energized and focused will make the class more fun and more effective.

Ditch the Cell Phones

A particular pitfall of teaching in the 21st century is that every student has a world-class distraction device in their pocket. It's not the end of the world if a student quickly checks their phone for important notifications, but you don't want half the students to be sitting in their seats, scrolling through social media. That's a tip-off that the energy has dropped, and that the students aren't very engaged (in addition to being extremely disrespectful).

If you catch students spending time on their phones during class, ask them to put their devices away. Some teachers even insist that students turn off their phones or leave them in a pile by the door so they can give the class their full focus.

Prohibit Coaching from Other Students

You may have "helpful" students who want to chime in with their own coaching during class. This can range from experienced players who want to offer advice before and after every exercise, to peers who see a student struggling and want to call out ideas and encouragement mid-scene. Don't allow this.

Allowing other students to coach—even if they are more experienced than you—undermines your teaching authority. It can also be highly confusing to students, as they start hearing different ideas from different voices. While these attempts to "backseat coach" are generally well-meaning, they're not helpful to you or your class. If more experienced students start giving feedback as though *they* are the teacher, stop their comments immediately.

Even more egregious are students who "coach" their class-mates in the middle of an exercise. It can be squirmy to watch someone struggling on stage, so sometimes other students will call out hints or ideas from their seats in the audience. You should immediately and directly request that this stop.

It's incredibly distracting and unhelpful to have students trying to add to your teaching. Be adamant about not allowing it. Regular offenders may need to be spoken to after class, or addressed by the theater's education director at your request.

How to Request That Students Stop Backseat Coaching

When unwanted coaching happens, you should interrupt and simply say, "Thank you, but let me do the coaching today." If that feels too direct, you can try something like, "I see you have a lot of ideas to offer, but would you mind if I did the coaching today?" (Search for *non-violent communications* for guidance on how to be direct without being confrontational.)

Watch the Time

As you're running your class, you should constantly be moni-toring the time. I often find that my sense of time vanishes when I'm wholly engaged in teaching; sometimes it will feel like we've been at things for hours and only twenty minutes have passed. Other times it seems like we've just started and there are only a few minutes left.

Keeping tabs on the time is important for several reasons. First, you want to make sure you get through your exercises in time to reach your end goal. You might need to cut an exercise short or reduce the number of students who do an individual exer-cise to ensure you have enough time to build your skills atop one another. You also want to leave enough time at the end for wrapping up and reflection. Finally, your students have lives and commitments and parking meters. At best, running long will inconvenience students; at worst, people will simply leave before you've ended the class. Respect everyone's time by not only starting your class promptly, but also ending promptly. (Tip: If you're teaching a longer class with a break in the middle, that break should come at a planned time, and not too early or late.)

If time management is a struggle for you, consider designating one student as a timekeeper and asking them to call out the time every twenty minutes. You can also download a free time-keeping app—workout "Tabata" apps are good for buzzing at regular intervals. Being up front with the class that you have a schedule and timing only emphasizes your authority and good preparation.

Chapter 11
Running Exercises

Exercises are the building blocks of your class. Stacked atop one another, they help your students put skills together to achieve your class goal. Each exercise also stands alone and has a beginning (explaining the exercise), middle (doing the exercise), and end (reflecting on the exercise). An exercise may be done only once—for instance, a group exercise where everyone participates simultaneously—or multiple times, where different pairs or trios get up to try. Running successful exercises will lead to an efficient and smooth class.

Introducing an Exercise

Every exercise should begin with a *clear* and *concise* explanation. If it takes more than a couple of sentences to explain, that's a sign that the exercise is too complicated and needs to be broken down into smaller component skills. Below are examples of a clear explanation and a not-so-clear explanation for an exercise:

Clear and Concise Explanation

We are going to have two people on stage. The first person will initiate by naming the location, for example "Welcome to the thrift store." The second person will then give a reason why they are at that location, for example, "I'm looking for a shirt to wear to a party."

Giving an example of "naming the location" is helpful for the above exercise. Without an example to reference, the instructions might be harder to understand:

Concise but Unclear Explanation

We are going to have two people on stage. The first person will initiate by naming the location. The second person will give a reason why they are at that location.

To a new student, the phrase "naming the location" may be unclear. Should the name be something like "Bob" or more like "Casa Morgenstern"? A quick example can help clarify. But beware over-explaining:

Over-Explained

We are going to have two people on stage. The first person will initiate by naming the location, for example: "Welcome to the thrift store" or "Thanks for visiting my law firm." The second person will then give a reason why they are at that location, for example: "I am looking for a shirt to wear to a party" or "I was in a car accident and need a lawyer." Remember that we can explicitly name the location by using the name in our response, or we can describe the things that

you might do at the location. For example, you could say
"Your tee time is coming up" to name the location as a golf
course, or you could say "We'll be landing in thirty
minutes" to establish the location as an airplane. Don't
forget you can also use physicality to establish the location,
such as paddling a boat to help establish that you are on
some kind of body of water. Are there any questions?

This is too much detail and too many options. Students are likely going to get lost or get into their heads about all the different ways they could approach the exercise.

Give your exercise *just* enough explanation and see what your students discover. You can always interject more coaching in the middle of the exercise rather than giving all the possibilities up front and at once. You also want to be specific about exactly what you are looking for. If students are confused, it's likely because you haven't been crisp enough on the goal of the exercise or adequately explained what success looks like. Let's go over a few more examples:

Unclear Explanation

One person will make a statement and the other person will
react to that statement.

This explanation lacks detail and opens the door to confusion. What does "react to that statement" mean? A physical reaction? An emotional reaction? A verbal response? An opinion? If the goal is for students to show both a physical and emotional reaction without speaking, it might be better explained as:

Clear, Concise Explanation

One person will make a statement and the other person will show, physically and emotionally, how they are reacting, without speaking.

It may also be helpful to reinforce the *why* behind an exercise. In some cases, the *why* may be obvious, as it directly relates to the topic of your class. But often, reminding people can help make an exercise clearer:

Clear, Concise Explanation + the Why

One person will make a statement and the other person will show physically and emotionally how they are reacting without speaking. Remember that emotion can carry as much power as words and help make our scenes richer and less talky.

Physically embodying the exercise as you're describing it is another way to make sure your explanation is clear. If you are describing an exercise between two people, physically stand on one side of the stage as you describe what the first student would do, then step over to where the second student would stand to describe what that person would do.

If the exercise involves entrances, exits, or any other specific physical choices, move through the space as you describe those components. This will better help the students visualize what you're describing. (True story: I once took a class on edits where the teacher described each edit in words instead of physically demonstrating. It was ... confusing.) *Show, don't tell* is always good advice.

Once you've clearly and concisely explained the exercise, you're ready to get started. You should be able to tell pretty quickly if the students understood correctly or if they're confused. If they're not doing the exercise correctly, stop and give additional clarifications, then restart.

If the first people to try an exercise get it wrong, I like to allow them to re-do the exercise from the beginning, with my improved instructions. And I like to thank them for being the "guinea pigs." Put the blame on yourself. It's not the students who failed; it was you who failed to explain clearly.

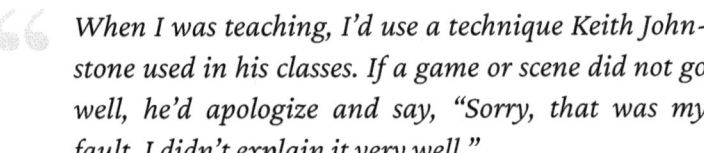

> *When I was teaching, I'd use a technique Keith Johnstone used in his classes. If a game or scene did not go well, he'd apologize and say, "Sorry, that was my fault, I didn't explain it very well."*
>
> — Dick Chudnow

The Importance of Side Coaching

Side coaching means gently correcting and steering exercises *while they are happening* to help students learn and be successful. You *must* side coach. But like wasabi, a little side coaching goes a long way; too much is easily overwhelming.

Learning to side coach gracefully and effectively will be one of the biggest challenges of your teaching career and key to determining your success. The practice is critical because learning to improvise is all about building new neural pathways in the brain—just like learning to drive a car, play guitar, or speak a foreign language. A student's improv journey progresses from thinking too much and making conscious decisions ("I need to remember to agree here") to making autonomous decisions *without* overthinking (just naturally agreeing). In teaching people to improvise, you're helping to move their reactions from the conscious to the subconscious.

To build these new neural pathways, it's important for students to repeatedly do things correctly. Allowing students to repeatedly do things the wrong way will build incorrect neural pathways in the brain. These bad habits, done over and over, can become ingrained.

This does not mean you should stop and correct every single thing a student does wrong. There is value in letting students try to work through challenges; side coaching every line in a scene soon becomes exhausting and frustrating for the student. But far too many teachers do little or *no* side coaching, and instead try to deconstruct the mistakes of the exercise after it has ended—which isn't nearly as helpful.

Imagine you were taking a Spanish class instead of an improv class. If you started using the word "embarazada" for "embarrassed," the teacher would (hopefully) stop you immediately and correct you. They would inform you that "embarazada" actually means "pregnant," and that you were using the incorrect word. Letting you continue to say the wrong word until the end of the exercise would only reinforce the error in your brain, making it harder to learn and associate the correct word.

Don't let students muddle through a painful scene, doing poor improv—or directly contradicting the goal of the exercise—and only *afterwards* talk about all the things that should have been different. Instead, you must side coach in the moment to gently redirect students into building good neural pathways. Done skillfully, side coaching gently guides exercises back on track, helps students learn, and gives them a feeling of success.

Nudges, Not Hammers

Think of side coaching as giving the rudder a tiny nudge, rather than taking over as the pilot. Done ham-handedly, side coaching can destroy the flow of an exercise, frustrate students, and prevent them from learning because the teacher is doing too much of the steering.

Your goal is to find the sweet spot—where you are the trusted guide, nudging students in the right direction, helping them make better choices without telling them what those choices should be. Side coaching is one of the harder things you'll learn as an improv teacher, so give yourself grace as you're building this skill. You're learning, too!

 When I was a rookie improvisor, Kent McCarty had us doing scene starts. The suggestion was "pressure," and the other player in my scene started by flicking a pressure gauge and saying, "500 PSI! Uh oh, it's never gone that high before." I responded by saying "YEAH! New record!" and held up my hand for a high-five, thinking that was funny.

Kent stopped the scene and said: "Sure, that's yes-and. But is there any truth in that? Who would ever respond to a crisis that way?" We replayed the scene with the same opening line, except I responded with concern, and the rest of it was golden.

Because he stopped and coached in the moment, it immediately and permanently changed how I viewed improvising.

— Bill Cernansky

Avoid "Choice Coaching"

One pitfall to avoid is "choice coaching"—going beyond gentle nudging and actually telling the students what choices to make in the scene. An example of gentle nudging would be saying, "Add some information," while choice coaching would sound more like "Tell her you're a cowboy and that's why you're selling hats." In the first case, you're helping the student to realize that they have done the "yes" but not the "and." In the second case, you're literally writing the scene for them.

As an experienced improviser (and an outside observer) you will no doubt have your own ideas about what the "right" move looks like. Often you may see a fun game that students missed or have a brilliant idea for the next beat of the scene. But it's not your job to tell the students what *your* ideas are or what *you* would have done; it's your job to help them practice finding a better choice, even if their choice is a bit mundane for your taste.

The best side coaching focuses on the *what*, not the *how*. Good side coaching sounds like:

"React..."

"Edit..."

"Don't lose your character..."

You might be choice coaching if you say things like:

"Burst into tears."

"Cut to the schoolyard and do a scene where everyone is playing hopscotch except for Deandre."

"Come in as a pirate."

Setting Student Expectations

Your students may have never experienced side coaching, so they may be surprised when you do it. For this reason, it can be helpful to briefly explain what it will entail before you begin. Simply say something like:

> *"I may interject with some quick coaching while you're doing exercises. Try to remain focused in the exercise and continue. It doesn't mean you're doing anything wrong— I'm just helping you to see other possibilities."*

While new students will likely be unfamiliar with side coaching, you may be surprised by the number of veteran students who have not experienced it either. I once taught at an established theater where none of the students (many of them long-time mainstage players) had ever been side coached.

Your Reactions Matter (a Lot)

As you teach, students will constantly look and listen to gauge your reactions. It's important to remain positive and to *visibly* and *audibly* show your appreciation for what they are doing at all times. Smile. Clap your hands. Exclaim "Good!" or "Great!" And if you can, laugh! (As a teacher, your bar for laughing should be *very* low. Fake a laugh if you can do so convincingly.) When students see that the teacher is enjoying the class, it gives them confidence and a feeling of achievement.

If things are not going well, never show frustration or disappointment. It's important to remain unrelentingly upbeat and positive, even when students are doing terrible improv. If the teacher seems dispirited, it will send students down a spiral of shame and torpedo their confidence. Even a less-than-successful exercise should end with clapping it up for the participants. Don't let people slink off stage feeling like they've failed.

Your side coaching attitude is as important as the words that you say. The tone of your voice should be authoritative but casual. Friendly. Positive. You're conveying, "Here's an idea that might help," not, "This is terrible and you're doing it wrong."

Try to keep a smile in your voice!

> *I was in a class taught by Starr Ahrens and every time I glanced at her while people were performing, she looked like she could not wait to see what was going to happen next. It was very encouraging.*
>
> — Hadas Cassorla

Chapter 12
The Mechanics of Side Coaching

Gaining confidence with side coaching takes practice. It can feel rude or awkward to interject new direction or interrupt scenes with corrections. Functionally, side coaching comes in three different forms:

- Quick interjections
- Pause/continue
- Stop/diagnose/rewind

Quick Interjections

Most side coaching should be the first type—quick interjections that don't pause the action. This is the equivalent of gently nudging the steering wheel. Something has been missed, a student made a poor choice, an offer was dropped. As quickly as possible, you interject to help the student make a different choice:

> **Mae:** *"It's time for your bath."*
> **Jonas:** *"No, it's not."*

Teacher: *"Let's agree."*
Jonas: *"I've got my rubber ducky."*

If you can nudge the exercise with a word or a short phrase, there's no need to stop the scene. Here's another example of a simple, quick interjection to help guide things back on track:

Taylor: *"Look at that!"*
Parker: *"I've never seen anything like that before."*
Taylor: *"Should we touch it?"*
Parker: *"I'm afraid."*
Teacher: *"Name the thing."*
Parker: *"It's a giant lizard."*

Notice how in this example, the teacher gives the students a few lines to see if they can achieve the goal, rather than side coaching immediately. But once it becomes clear that the students are not going to name the thing, the teacher gently reminds them with a quick interjection that doesn't harm the flow of the scene.

Side coaching is all about nudging a scene back on track. We want to avoid explaining *why* we're coaching. The *why* behind the exercise should be covered during the introduction. Add too much justification, and you can interrupt the flow of the exercise and make it hard for the students to continue, as shown in this next example:

Taylor: *"Look at that!"*
Parker: *"I've never seen anything like that before."*
Taylor: *"Should we touch it?"*
Parker: *"I'm afraid."*

Teacher: *"Name the thing. It's important in scenes that we clearly name anything we are talking about, so we avoid vague scenes where neither the players nor the audience know what we're talking about. It's okay to make bold choices—you don't have to wait for your scene partner to do so."*
Taylor: *"Uh..."*

The best interjections are usually just a word or a quick phrase:

"Agree."

"Respond to what she just said."

"Can you heighten?"

"Find your edit."

"Sing louder."

Students can hear and act on these coaching cues in the moment without stepping out of the flow of the scene. With practice, you'll be able to use an economy of words to gently correct and steer students in the right direction. Remember, you're nudging *them* to figure out the right answer, not giving them the answer. Avoid telling them the right choice:

Taylor: *"Look at that!"*
Parker: *"I've never seen anything like that before."*
Taylor: *"Should we touch it?"*
Parker: *"I'm afraid."*
Teacher: *"How about making it a giant lizard."*
Parker: *"It's a giant lizard."*

Oops! We accidentally veered into choice coaching by giving them an answer.

What If You Miss the Moment to Interject?

Sometimes you will miss a necessary side coaching moment. It may be because the students were talking so fast that you didn't have a chance to interject, or it may be that you simply didn't catch the misstep when it happened. If it feels like *not* making the correction will harm the exercise or the students' learning, you may still be able to interject:

> **Seth:** *"We're almost on the surface of the moon."*
> **Olga:** *"No, we're not."*
> **Seth:** *"Yes, we are; the altimeter says five feet."*
> **Teacher:** *"Olga, try agreeing with Seth."*
> **Olga:** *"You're right, we're at five feet."*

Even though you didn't correct Olga *at the moment* she made the denial, it's still close enough that she's able to redirect and the scene can continue without devolving into an argument.

Pause/Rewind/Continue

If too much time has passed between the error and your correction, you may need to pause the scene and rewind before continuing:

> **Zach:** *"The barn is on fire."*
> **Amahl:** *"We're out of milk."*
> **Zach:** *"Now we can't have breakfast."*
> **Amahl:** *"I'll go to the store."*
> **Teacher:** *"Pause. Zach initiated the scene with 'The barn is*

on fire' but we never acknowledged that. Let's rewind and take it from there. Zach, say your first line again."
Zach: *"The barn is on fire."*
Amahl: *"Oh my goodness, we have to save the horses!"*

If you need to rewind, very clearly and loudly say, "Pause," make your correction, and restart as quickly and gracefully as possible.

> *"Pause. We seem stuck in a negotiation. Can you move the scene forward?"*

> *"Pause. We established that Kelsey is a werewolf but that's been dropped."*

> *"Pause. We need to give focus."*

Helping Students Help Themselves

Often, students aren't listening to their scene partners (or themselves). In this case, instead of telling them exactly what they missed, see if they can figure it out:

> **Ani:** *"I got a new haircut."*
> **Maximo:** *"I failed my driving test."*
> **Teacher:** *"Pause. Maximo, do you remember what Ani said to you?"*
> **Maximo:** *"Um, she got a new haircut?"*
> **Teacher:** *"Right! Let's respond to that."*
> **Maximo:** *"Your new haircut looks great!"*

In other cases, see if students can diagnose where they've gotten stuck rather than telling them the answer:

Pedro: *"Here's a basketball."*
Shayne: *"Toss it to me."*
Pedro: *"Toss it back."*
Shayne: *"Let's practice dribbling."*
Pedro: *"Look, I'm dribbling."*
Teacher: *"Pause. Why is this scene stuck?"*
Shayne: *"We're doing an activity instead of having relationships."*
Teacher: *"Yes!"*
Pedro: *"My mom used to play basketball with me when I was a kid, but she died."*

Stop/Diagnose/Rewind

Sometimes, an exercise goes completely off the rails and both you (and likely the students) know that it's not working. Follow your instincts and pause the scene to see if you can figure it out. Take a beat to try and diagnose what went wrong:

> *"Pause. It feels like this isn't working. Can anybody say why?"*

Once you've diagnosed the problem, either continue the exercise (with corrections) or call amnesty and start over. It doesn't do the students any favors to continue muddling through an exercise that is clearly not working.

Occasionally, you may need to stop an exercise that has just gotten off to a bad start. Some instances of bad starts include:

- A scene began with an argument and, after thirty seconds, is still swirling around in circles

- Subject matter of questionable taste that nobody really wants to watch
- A musical game where all the players are completely off the rhythm
- Any exercise where the students are simply not doing what you asked

Yes, you want to allow students the opportunity to work their way through problems on stage; after all, during a show, there won't be someone to side coach them. But once an exercise has veered too far off course, the odds of the students fixing it are low. The negative returns to fighting through a bad exercise far outweigh the learning opportunity. **Remember: you want to prevent students from building negative neural pathways in their brains.** Sometimes, the best thing you can do is stop an exercise, admit that it's gone wonky, shake it out, and start again with light correction and a completely new suggestion.

If you do have to stop an exercise that isn't working, always do so with a smile. It should not feel like the students have failed. Make your corrections and then give them a chance to try again. Never cut an exercise short and send the students off stage without giving them a chance to re-do the exercise successfully.

Make Students Do the Exercises Right

It's important that the students perform exercises correctly. If they don't, they risk not learning the skill that you're trying to teach. Students may do an exercise wrong for one of several reasons:

- They don't understand the instructions
- They don't have the skills to complete the exercise
- They're learning
- They're being a smarty-pants

They Don't Understand the Instructions

Perhaps your directions were unclear, or what you were looking for was too vague. This happens a lot, which is why carefully thinking through the intention of each exercise and being crisp about what you're trying to achieve is critical. Here's an example of an explanation that isn't quite clear:

> *"One student is going to initiate with a statement and the second student is going to respond non-verbally."*

This might be crystal clear in your head, but not to the students:

Jeanette: *"I failed my algebra test."*
Piotr: *(Gasps)*
Teacher: (Pausing the exercise) *"We're going for non-verbal responses."*
Piotr: *"I thought non-verbal meant no spoken words."*

In this case, the teacher actually meant for the player to respond with a *physical* choice, but by providing poorly phrased direction, they confused the students and weren't clear on what they were looking for.

They Don't Have the Skills to Complete the Exercise

You may ask students to complete an exercise involving necessary underlying skills that they haven't yet learned. In this case, you should back up to that underlying skill in order to develop a building block for success.

For example, let's say you're teaching an Armando class, and you've designed an exercise to start new scenes inspired by the monologue. If you haven't properly built the skill of editing, the students won't know how to wipe one scene in order to execute their new scene starts. You'll need to first spend some time reviewing editing skills.

They're Learning

In an ideal situation, a student does an exercise wrong, you make a correction, and then they do it right.

Here are the instructions:

> *"One student is going to initiate a scene, and the second student will establish the location where the scene takes place."*

And this is the scene:

> **Siobhan:** *"We got the chocolate delivery."*
> **Sebastian:** *"Please put it on the counter."*
> **Teacher:** *"We need to be specific about the location. We don't know where the counter is."*
> **Sebastian:** *"Please put it on the counter here in the confectionary shop."*

Some teachers might miss this correction, because you *could* argue that "the counter" is a location or that "on the counter" implies that we are in a kitchen or a store. But assuming the whole point of this exercise is to be *specific* about the location, the student's first response falls short. You won't do them any favors by letting this one go.

They Are Being a Smarty-Pants

Some students just have to see if they can get away with not doing your exercise the right way. They'll make a joke, find a loophole in your instructions, or interpret the goal of the exercise in a clever way. In improv, we call this "finding the game." It's great in a show, but not helpful in a class where you have a specific goal for each skill.

Don't let smarty-pants students undermine your authority by monkeying with your exercises. An unexpected approach is great *only* if it still accomplishes what you want the exercise to accomplish. If it doesn't, make them do it the right way.

A laugh doesn't mean it's right

Doing an exercise the wrong way oftentimes gets a laugh. Be sure not to confuse getting a laugh with doing it right. In a show, getting a laugh by breaking the "rules" of the game may be exactly what the format needs. But in a classroom setting, where you're trying to help students build skills, substituting laughs for learning is never the right answer.

As the teacher, you can acknowledge that the rule-breaking was funny and enjoyable, but also reinforce that it didn't match the aim of the exercise; they should try again.

When Your Exercise Isn't Working

It happens—you start an exercise and it just doesn't work. The students don't get it, they can't do it correctly, or the way you've structured it doesn't make sense. If you can't fix it on the fly, you may need to nix the exercise and move on to your next one (yet another reason to plan multiple exercises for each atomic skill).

If an exercise fails, the students mustn't feel that it's their fault. As the teacher, you should admit the exercise isn't working, take the blame, and move on. Don't power through if it's clearly not worth it. You can say:

> *"Hey, everyone, this exercise isn't quite working. It's my fault, so let's move on to the next thing. It's improv! Even teachers make mistakes."*

Coach One Skill at a Time

Overthinking is the biggest impediment for new improvisers. Since students can only focus on one thing at a time, it's important to limit your side coaching to the single skill you're working on in the moment. This can be challenging, because your students will likely make all kinds of mistakes that bear correction.

For example, you might be coaching a scene on character work, but your students are also asking lots of questions, blocking, or failing to establish relationships.

You have to let a lot of mistakes go in order to focus on the primary goal of the exercise.

- In an exercise focusing on agreement, you shouldn't *also* coach students on their character choices.
- In an exercise focusing on object work, you shouldn't *also* coach on narrative.

- In an exercise focusing on edits, you shouldn't *also* coach on status.

Stopping to correct an exercise *every* time a student does something wrong will be frustrating and quickly get students into their heads.

The exception to this rule is when a small coaching adjustment can help an exercise get unstuck. In a character exercise, you likely shouldn't divert time coaching a student about asking questions—unless the student was repeatedly asking questions and preventing the scene from moving forward.

In this case, you could gently call out "questions" as a reminder. Similarly, if you were coaching a genre exercise focused on Shakespeare scenes, you should not interject to correct a student on a denial, unless that denial were threatening to derail the success of the exercise itself.

It can be hard to refrain from side coaching obvious student errors, but you must maintain focus on the key goal of the exercise. If the point of the exercise is to help a student gain comfort with using Shakespearean language (as it might be in the above example), interspersing additional coaching around basic improv tenets may be too much for them to process. One thing at a time.

Create "Wins"

Ultimately, your goal in coaching exercises should be to create "wins" in the minds of your students. Confidence breeds success and you want students to walk away from any exercise feeling as though they learned something. This could be because they did the exercise successfully, or because they learned from their mistakes and feel confident they can do better next time.

A lot of smiling, celebrating, and clapping should accompany every exercise. Celebrate anything that goes well, and even if something isn't successful, still show how proud you are that the student got up and attacked the exercise. We just talked about how you shouldn't correct errors unrelated to the intention of the exercise, but you should absolutely go out of your way to point out *good things* that students do, even if unrelated. Praise great initiations, fun characters, and unexpected, bold choices. You cannot offer too much praise as a teacher:

> *"Did you see how Angela had a strong emotional reaction to Vladimir's offer?"*

> *"I loved Shay's choice not to speak right away and give Ana the focus."*

> *"Freya's description of the garden tool as a 'two-dollar rake' was great specificity."*

You will likely end up praising things that students didn't consciously try to do. That's okay! Being singled out by the teacher for something they did well gives students a warm, fuzzy feeling and can keep them from beating themselves up on the drive home.

 In the first improv class I ever took with Scott Ingwersen we were doing warm-ups. When you messed up you had to say, "I failed," as though it was an accomplishment and take a bow, after which everyone

cheered. That ritual really helped dampen my internal critic and internal filter.

— Susan Weatherford Scoven

Give Good Notes

Giving notes is an important part of teaching, but it's something that many teachers struggle with. Sharing candid, constructive, direct feedback can initially feel uncomfortable and confrontational—especially if you haven't come from a work or family atmosphere where that is normalized.

Yet, withholding notes is not kind. Your job as the teacher is to help students improve, and they cannot do so if you fail to help them see where they can develop. You must deliver both positive and negative feedback to help people grow.

Here are some guidelines to help you deliver better notes:

Combine Positive and Negative Feedback

Find good things to note along with areas for improvement. Students will be more receptive to criticism if it is combined with praise. Don't just launch into all the things that went wrong in the exercise.

Be Clear Who the Note Is For

Sometimes, in trying to avoid singling out an individual, we fail to deliver a clear note:

UNCLEAR: *"It felt like some offers got dropped in the scene."*

DIRECT: *"Gigi, LaDawna said that there was a giant meteor heading for Earth, but you never responded to that."*

Don't Say That Bad Work Is Good

While we want to find things to praise, we also want to avoid claiming that obviously poor work is good. Students aren't dumb. If a scene is rambling and incoherent, find an element to praise without saying, "That was a great scene!"

Avoid Saying "Can't," "Don't," or Implying a Student Lacks Talent

It shouldn't be "You're bad at accents" or "You can't do a Scottish accent." It should be "Accents would be a great thing to work on" or "I bet you have an opportunity to learn more accents."

Words Like "Maybe," "Might," and "Could Have" Can Soften Feedback

There are no right or wrong choices in improv. You can give direct notes without making anything an absolute:

ABSOLUTE: *"Tim, you missed the edit after the third beat."*

DIRECT, BUT SOFTER: *"Tim, you might have had an opportunity to edit after the third beat."*

Consider Using "We" Instead of "You"

Improv is a team sport, and as the coach, you're part of the team. Using "we" language can help you take some of the responsibility:

YOU LANGUAGE: *"Jazmine, you denied Bill's offer of the office tour."*

WE LANGUAGE: *"Jazmine, it felt like we could have said yes to Bill's offer of the office tour."*

Avoid Value Judgements

Notes are simply your take on what could have been done differently. They needn't dwell on the outcome of the exercise.

BAD: *"We missed the chorus after the final verse and ruined the ending of the song."*

BETTER: *"We missed the chorus after the final verse, so we didn't get the big ending we love."*

Deliver Notes with a Smile

If you seem frustrated or angry, your notes will come off very differently than if you deliver them positively. The attitude should be, "Here are some things I noticed that you might find helpful." Not, "Here are all the terrible things that ruined the exercise."

It is often harder to deliver candid notes than it is to receive them. We imagine that people are going to be much more offended by our notes than they actually are. In truth, most people genuinely want to know what they can do to improve, and they value direct, candid, and kind feedback. Use soft language but be direct. Depending on the culture you grew up in, you may have scant experience delivering direct and candid feedback. This is a skill you will get better at over time, with practice.

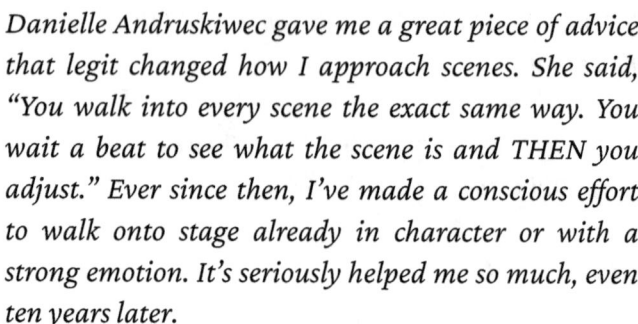 *Danielle Andruskiwec gave me a great piece of advice that legit changed how I approach scenes. She said, "You walk into every scene the exact same way. You wait a beat to see what the scene is and THEN you adjust." Ever since then, I've made a conscious effort to walk onto stage already in character or with a strong emotion. It's seriously helped me so much, even ten years later.*

— Emmy Serviss

Chapter 13
And, Scene! How to End Your Class

The last part of your syllabus should have dedicated time for students to practice putting their skills to use. This is where you've planned a few games, or a format, that lets them apply the skill in the kind of performance they would do in a show. Aim to leave at least fifteen minutes, or more if you have time.

A few tips:

- **Be thoughtful about picking games or formats that make the best use of the skill.** If your class was about sustaining longer scenes, this would probably not be the best class to end with quick-hit, gimmicky, short-form games.

- **Emphasize that you want students to practice the skill.** It's more important to focus on the skill itself than to get too wrapped up in the mechanics of the game or format.

- **Continue to side coach.** Don't let students forget about the skill they've just built.

- **Don't be discouraged if everyone isn't magically an expert at the skill.** Most improv skills take lots of practice for mastery. And remember that the brain works in funny ways: during sleep, our brains help us synthesize and store skills we learned earlier. Someone may not "get it" in class, only to come back a week later and have more success.

- **End on a high note.** If an exercise goes particularly well, that may be the best time to transition to the end of the class (but don't run the class long looking for that one final high note—sometimes it's not there).

Sooner than you think, it will be time to end the class. Start wrapping up early—you want to leave time for questions, discussion, and reflection at the end. It's not cool to keep students late. Respect their time just like you want them to respect yours. Even if everything is rocking and you sense that everyone is engaged and having a blast, be the teacher who ends on time.

Your End of Class Routine

You'll create your own ending routine, but this is what mine looks like:

Circle Everyone Up

Standing in a circle makes it easy to share reflections and have that last feeling of group togetherness. Start by sharing your appreciation for everyone's work in the class and giving posi-tive reinforcement.

Ask Students What They Learned

Go around the circle and ask people to say one thing they learned today. This is a chance to reinforce key points and find out if students had any breakthroughs. It's okay if students duplicate responses or can't think of anything. Some will have a nugget of gold!

Ask Students If They Have Questions or Observations

Sometimes students will want to dig deeper. This is your chance to let them do so. It's one reason to wrap up with plenty of time to spare. Tip: Saying "What questions do you have?" will elicit better responses than "Does anyone have any questions?"

Tell Students How to Contact You

Some teachers distribute personal business cards or share their social media handle. You may also direct students to reach you through the theater. No matter the method, make sure they know how to get in touch if they have further questions.

Offer Some Last Words of Encouragement

Leave students feeling positive about the class. Close by thanking the students and telling them you are proud of the work they did in class.

Offer to Post Class Notes (If You Can)

If there's a way for you to share your notes or offer a class handout, this can be a valuable takeaway. But don't promise notes if you aren't going to deliver. Be honest with yourself as to whether you're really going to sit down and write something up.

Close Class with Your Ritual of Choice

Don't just say, "I guess that's all," and have people wander away. Have your own group ritual for bringing the class to a close. Some teachers have the students clap in unison. Some teachers send a "beep" around the circle. My favorite close is to ask each student to think of one word that defined the class for them, then everyone puts their hands in the middle, counts to three, and shouts out that word. We finish with clapping it up.

After class, plan to stay for additional conversation. Some students may have questions or observations that they don't want to share with the full group. Some may just want to come up and thank you. Aim to make yourself available for this, and try to be the last person to leave.

Remember to Review Your Syllabus

Immediately after the class ends, quickly review your syllabus. Make note of what didn't work, what you had to skip, and what worked particularly well. It will be easier to teach this class in the future if you update your syllabus immediately to remind yourself what hit and what didn't.

You can also note certain talking points or questions that came up during the class. Add those talking points to the syllabus so you remember for next time (and so your students can read those points if you plan post and share your syllabus with the class).

You did it! You taught your first improv class. Yes, you!

Chapter 14
Working with Students

I f students were robots, teaching would be easy. You'd give instruction A to get output B. Repeat every week, and everyone becomes a brilliant improviser.

Needless to say, students are not robots. They're humans, and they come with all the fears, foibles, limitations, and surprises that you'd expect when you get any group of people into a room. What's more, most people in your improv class will be somewhere between slightly and *wildly* outside their comfort zone. All this combined will lead you to realize that being an improv teacher is a lot like being a psychologist. Every student has a unique history, their own headspace, and their own challenges. There's no one-size-fits-all approach. Much of your job will be finding just the right words, exercises, praise, and challenges to meet each person where they are.

It's not easy.

While one student may thrive on being pushed hard, another may shut down and refuse to participate after a gentle correction. One reluctant student may secretly want you to make them get up on stage while another reluctant student may not come back the next week. And a student who seemed like an angel in one class can suddenly turn into a monster the following week if they have a fight with their girlfriend or a threatening phone call from their landlord weighing on them.

Just as improvisers have to constantly listen, observe, and react to do good scenes, teachers must do the same to coach, inspire, and manage their students. Done right, you can make a profound difference in people's lives. Done ham-handedly, you can lose the trust of the class.

In this chapter, we'll look at some of the different types of students you may encounter, along with tips to help them thrive—or, in some cases, help you survive.

Students Learn in Different Ways and at Different Speeds

There's no single, universally effective teaching method when it comes to how people learn:

- Some students learn faster by watching.
- Some students learn faster by doing.
- Some students learn immediately and then forget the next week.
- Some students take weeks to grasp a concept, but then have it forever.
- Some students cannot understand a verbal explanation of an exercise and have to see it to get it.
- Some students can watch an exercise for ten minutes and then still not understand it.
- Some students can hear you say something repeatedly, but it will only "click" when another teacher says it.

It can be frustrating that not every student learns the same way. You may feel like you're failing or that they're not trying hard enough. What worked last week might not work this week.

That's what happens when you deal with people. People are messy.

Until you've learned how your students learn, try to have grace and do *just enough*. Explain *just enough* for most students to understand your exercise, but don't over-explain trying to cater to the visual learners. They'll pick it up when they see it. Encourage someone *just enough* to come up and try an exercise they're fearful of, but not so much that they shut down or cry. And give students *just enough* tries at an exercise to get it right, but not so much that they feel like they're repeatedly failing. Praise them and let them try it again the next week.

Put on your psychologist hat, be flexible, and realize that each person may need something a little bit different.

> *I was taking my first improv class from Sid Grossfeld in Los Angeles. I was a funny guy, but whenever I did anything, he'd yell: "SCHTICK!" This happened three or four times, until he said stop thinking and just go along with what someone else is doing. It worked. I got it. It was my AHA moment. I fell in love with improv then. What could be better than not having to think, not having to come up with "Schtick."*
>
> — Dick Chudnow

Teaching Beginners

In any class for beginners, you're likely to have a wide range of skills, ages, and motivations. A significant number of people live in daily fear of being asked to share a "fun fact" about themselves. You have the awesome opportunity (and responsibility) to start a student's improv journey on the right foot.

The most important thing with beginners is to bring them along *slowly*. You're likely to have people in class who are deeply fearful, who have a phobia of public speaking, or who have never even been up on a stage in front of a group before. A talented (and now fearless) improviser once told me about sitting in the parking lot for a full thirty minutes before her first improv class, trying to will herself to step out of the car.

For someone brand-new to improv, a "win" may be as simple as:

- Walking in the door.
- Taking off their jacket (I've seen beginners on stage in full parkas and hats as a protective barrier).
- Standing in a circle.
- Saying their name in front of the group.

With new improvisers, you need to slow down and give them a chance to get comfortable with speaking in a group setting. You may not want to put beginners alone on stage in their first class. It's like acclimating a kitten to a new home. Let them be in the space and sniff around a bit before getting into improv exercises.

You'll find that beginners struggle with basic things, like hearing what their scene partner is saying. And I don't mean they can't listen; I mean they literally can't hear because they are so in their own heads, or their hearts are beating too fast. It's up to you to make the situation as non-threatening as possible. Consider allowing them to do their first exercises in pairs and without an audience. Or perhaps in groups of four, where nobody feels like they're being put on the spot?

Beginners *especially* need wins and praise. Make exercises easy and achievable, and praise everyone. It should be impossible to "fail" in the first few classes. It's better to go slow and learn less than to frustrate students and confirm their worst fears about improv class being too hard or too scary.

A lot of what beginning students do looks like warm-up games, not performance skills. That's okay! Getting newbies into a playful headspace that's more about laughing with a group than "doing improv" will lay a foundation for the skill work you'll introduce later.

 My teacher would always say, "Cheers is not a show about a bar." I think about that often. It helps me keep in mind that characters and their relationship to each other are more important than the setting. One of the reasons it stuck so much is that she repeated that A LOT during the Intro to Improv class.

— Dan Lamm

Caring for Fearful Students

Although beginning students are often more noticeably fearful, the truth is that you will have fearful students at every level. Even in your mainstage rehearsals, expect that many performers are secretly nervous about getting up and taking risks in front of their peers.

Fearful students will try to talk themselves out of going up on stage, and the best way to help them is by preventing their internal bargaining. That's why I almost always call students up myself (often by picking names out of a hat). If left to self-select, the fearful students will talk themselves out of going up. If the teacher makes the choice, it's easier for the student and it takes the pressure off.

Most of the time this works, and the reluctant student will smile shyly and then come up on stage to do the exercise. But occasionally, a student will flat-out refuse. You'll need to make a quick determination: do they simply need an extra nudge, or are they so petrified that putting them on stage is going to lead to a breakdown?

Some ways you can nudge include:

- **Offer to send someone else up with them.** For instance, in a singing class, send up someone to duet instead of making it a solo. Or if there's another student who was fearful before, ask if they'll go up for support.

- **Remember your blockers.** If you gently ask why they don't want to go up and they mention one of your blockers, this is a great time to use your blocker removal: *"Don't worry about not being able to do a British accent. That's not required for Shakespeare at all. Did you ever see Baz Luhrmann's* Romeo + Juliet?*"*

- **Tell them they can stop at any time.** Sometimes they just need to know they have an out: *"Tell you what, let's try doing one and if it's not fun you can stop any time."*

If the student still refuses—or they seem like they're about to melt down—just gracefully move on to the next person and don't belabor trying to get them up onto stage. It won't do them any good if you shame them, push too hard, or get the rest of the students to chant their name. I do recommend you talk privately with the student after class to check in and see how they're feeling. They might need a word of encouragement or want to tell you about something going on in their life.

All that said, some people can take a while to come out of their shell. Gently encourage but never push too hard. Let people gain confidence at their own pace.

Managing Classes at Different Levels

Often, you'll have students with very different skill levels in the same class. Whether it's a beginner class or an advanced class, it's likely that the range of abilities and experience will be quite broad. It's up to you to figure out how to give each student the best possible class.

Here are some strategies:

- **Try to find the middle ground on exercises.** If you cater your exercises to the least-experienced students, you'll find that the more-experienced students get bored. At the same time, running exercises that are only going to be achievable by your advanced students could leave the less-experienced students behind. Try to split the difference and run exercises that are neither too easy nor too hard.

- **Pitch your corrections and side coaching to the individual.** Advanced students may warrant more intensive side coaching than newer students who have fewer skills. Something that you "let go" with a less-experienced student may be something that you call out for an advanced student. Similarly, you may find that you have to side coach a newer student on basic improv skills to ensure they can keep the exercise going.

- **Pair up people with similar skill sets.** Exercises may be more achievable if you put students together who have similar abilities...

- **Or mix and match skill sets.** It may help to mix up skill sets, letting the less-experienced students benefit from playing with advanced students and challenging the experienced students to support beginner players.

Sometimes, you will start teaching a class and realize that the entire group is at a much more basic level than the material you have planned. This often happens when the requirements for an "Intermediate" or "Advanced" class are unclear or unenforced. In this case, you may have to scrap your entire syllabus and focus on more basic work. You can also remain in just the rudimentary atomic skills you prepared, without moving on to the more advanced work.

On the flip side, sometimes you've planned a lot of basic work and you discover that the class is much more advanced. In that case, move on quickly to the harder work. It's better to give students the class they need than to stubbornly insist on the class you planned.

Supporting Students with Disabilities

Improv is for everyone. Generally, students are extremely supportive of classmates with disabilities. If your class has students with disabilities, you should always view this as an opportunity, not as a problem. You'll just need to gracefully create accommodations to help everyone succeed.

Many improv games and exercises are about performing under constraints ("Do the scene, but you can only speak in sentences of five words..."). Accommodating players with disabilities is just playing with additional constraints.

Keep in mind that although games and formats have "rules," none of these are *actual* rules. Every single game and format can be modified to accommodate the abilities of the players. Just because there's a way your theater or team usually does something doesn't mean that's the right way or the only way. Be creative!

If you can't modify a game, exercise, or format to accommodate everyone in the class, discard it and choose something different. The person with the disability may gracefully offer to sit it out, but everything you do in class should be achievable by *every* student.

Here are some common disabilities you might encounter:

Physical Disabilities

Students may have limitations on mobility—walking, standing, and entering or exiting the stage. Any game or format can be played seated instead of standing. A non-mobile student can "enter" a scene by speaking and the more-mobile students can move the scene to them (rather than them moving to the scene). Short-form games with a physical aspect can be modified to use only arms, only legs, or even just a verbal component.

Hearing Loss

Students with limited hearing may need an interpreter or require the other students to speak loudly or speak only in one ear. Group scenes may be particularly difficult when there are a lot of loud voices at once; this may be an opportunity to work on focus exercises, so only one person is talking at a time.

Visual Impairment

Except for games with visual clue-giving, any game or format is easily achievable for students with limited vision. They will likely be able to tell you how comfortable they are moving around on the stage, and you can adjust accordingly. Students may need to take focus verbally when physically entering the scene, or describe more obviously the physical moves they're making ("Here's that cup of coffee you ordered").

Brain Injuries or Cognitive Limitations

A student with limited cognition can still be a part of any class. They may need your help to simplify exercises. Success for them may look different than for other students. It's a great opportunity for fellow students to support and "yes-and" their peer.

Autism Spectrum Disorder (ASD)

Improv can be profoundly helpful for students on the autism spectrum, as it gives concrete practice interacting with other people in a safe, supportive environment. You may find that some of these students struggle with emotional work but thrive on exercises that require memory, connections, or facts. Students on the spectrum may not read nuance well, so your coaching needs to be very direct. Don't hint at things you'd like them to do; give direction specifically. Use concrete (not abstract) language. Keep in mind that there is a lot of variation here, and each individual will present differently.

Attention Deficit Hyperactivity Disorder (ADHD)

ADHD can manifest in a number of different ways, from inattention and difficulty focusing, to hyperactivity (excessive fidgeting, restlessness, talking too much) to impulsivity. A student with ADHD may have trouble focusing on the exercise at hand, might find themselves needing to stand up and move around the room, or might distract the class with excessive talking and commenting. If you suspect ADHD in a student, and they are being disruptive, your best bet is a friendly (but firm) request for them to focus. Don't assume they are being inattentive or distracting out of disrespect. You can accommodate their needs by giving them space and permission to stand in the back, take a break from the class, or use whatever fidget device they prefer.

 I was in a Harold class with Bill Cernansky and I was new and nervous and chatty. At one point he just stopped the class and asked me to control my excitement out of respect for the rest of the class.

It was very nicely done and I think probably out of understanding of an ADHD mindset. But it really stuck with me how sincere and firm he was about

calling me out. Like, he got control of the class (read:
me) without making me feel bad.

— Hadas Cassorla

Students with disabilities know they have a disability and
don't need you to make a big deal about it. But that doesn't
mean you should ignore it, either. They're the ones who know
best what kind accommodations they need, so don't hesitate
to ask what will help them be more successful and comfortable. Don't assume that they'll tell you without being asked.

At the same time, students with disabilities may not always
feel comfortable disclosing their disability status to you, or
may ask for accommodations without explanation. It's up to
you to gracefully look, listen, and recognize when students
need accommodation. And always look for ways to build
toward their strengths.

This is just a very brief overview of accommodating students
with disabilities. Use other teachers, internet groups, and your
best judgement to ensure you're taking care of everyone and
making each student a full participant in the class.

Dealing with Uncomfortable or Improper Behavior

It's your job to make sure that class is a safe space at all times.
If students make choices that don't honor this code—or if
anything happens in an exercise that makes people uncomfortable—you must stop things immediately and make a correction. Off-limits actions can include sexual content, violence,
politics, unwarranted touching or physicality, or anything
where you sense discomfort in the room and among the
participants.

Students may take exercises into foul territory for any of several reasons:

- They are nervous and the wrong thing just popped out.
- They think that being "edgy" is funny.
- Somebody made accidental innuendo and things snowballed from there.
- The person is genuinely trying to make people uncomfortable.
- The person is trying to be lecherous to their fellow students.

Whether it was accidental or intentional, the moment you recognize an exercise veering into improper material, immediately stop and redirect the exercise. How you do this depends on how egregious the violation was.

For example, if you sense that somebody got nervous and the wrong thing popped out, you can simply side coach with, "Let's make a different choice." After the exercise, you may want to discuss why you asked them to change what they said or did and remind the class about the consent and content guidelines that you discussed at the beginning of class.

If what was said or done was a more egregious violation of the class standards, stop the exercise immediately and have that discussion on the spot. To create an atmosphere of safety, something that's a significant violation warrants immediate discussion. Explain again about consent and how the class is a safe space for everyone. Even if two students in a scene consent to specific content, that doesn't mean that everyone else in the classroom consents to watching it. Be firm that this inappropriate content has no place in your class.

Sometimes a scene may veer into territory that doesn't specifi-cally violate the class content standards, but is nonetheless uncomfortable for the participants. If students are being humiliated, degraded, or otherwise put into unpleasant situa-tions, redirect or stop the exercise.

Students may not know how to protect themselves in scenes. They may believe that they are required to agree to anything that happens on stage. It's your job to protect them, not wait to see if they can extricate themselves from an uncomfort-able situation. Waiting to see if someone can execute a "status shift" while they're being degraded doesn't do anybody any favors. YOU are there to take care of your students and to give them confidence that they will be safe at all times.

It's better to be overly cautious and stop *anything* that doesn't feel right. If you let little things go, some students will want to see how far they can push the content. It's easy for a class to spiral into off-color territory. While some students genuinely enjoy "adult-themed" comedy, others may silently feel uncom-fortable or embarrassed. Your job is to be the buzzkill who keeps the class out of the gutter.

Repeat Violators

If someone in your class repeatedly brings in improper content and violates the class standards, you should ask them to leave and have a follow-up discussion with them outside class. You should also bring in your theater director or event leader to discuss consequences.

As improvisors, we tend to err on the side of niceness. In this case, for the sake of everyone in the class, it's better to ask frequent or egregious offenders to go away.

Helping "In-Their-Head" Students

Sometimes we give students so much to think about in an exercise that they get stuck in their own heads and can no longer improvise. Students may stammer, struggle, or even completely shut down on stage and be unable to say *anything*.

If a student gets to this point, the best thing you can do is give them a graceful out and let them sit down to regroup. Continuing to push likely won't work. Telling a student "Just say anything" isn't helpful when they are so in their own head. Their brains are spinning so fast they can't stop and make any words come out.

Instead, take the blame—"My fault, I over-coached you"—and let them take a break before trying again. Ideally, get them back up again before the end of the class to have a win. If their brains are truly fried, you may find that they are done for the day. Afterward, if possible, chat with them and reiterate that it's not their fault—*you* as the coach didn't do a good enough job of helping them be successful.

The longer you teach, the better you'll get at recognizing when you've pushed someone close to the breaking point. Learn to avoid the "brain-fry zone."

Dealing With "the Jokester"

Ah, the jokester—the student who tries to find the loophole in every exercise and who can't help breaking the reality of the scene for a funny quip or comment. Jokesters are often very popular with their classmates, even as they're torpedoing your exercises and breaking the scenes.

Don't let them win.

Remind them that a laugh at the expense of the reality of the scene ultimately hurts them and their scene partners. Doing an exercise "wrong" for the sake of being funny isn't helping them learn. Make them do the exercise again the right way.

The challenge with jokesters is that they seem successful because they're getting laughs. After all, isn't the goal of improv to be funny?

This is a teaching moment for the whole class. Celebrate how funny that student is but also remind them that making jokes isn't the same thing as doing good improv.

I was a nervous student for the first four levels of improv school, always feeling a strong need to make our teacher laugh. "Follow the funny" became every-thing. But for me, it just wasn't clicking. Then one day, I attended a workshop with a visiting improviser. He started the session by repeating, at least three times (yep) that HE DID NOT WANT US TO BE FUNNY. All of a sudden, my shoulders relaxed. The relief was palpable. And in my final scene with a friend that day, I actually burst into song when the lines turned into a phrase from a popular song. The scene ended and my teacher, who was in the work-shop, rushed up and hugged me amidst the applause. When the visitor asked "Why the fuss?" she said, "It finally clicked!" But really, it was the pressure that had come off. It was so freeing.

— Kathy Rinaldi

Surviving Students Who Aren't Serious About Learning

Not everyone in your class may be interested in learning. Sometimes people take the class because they got a gift certificate. Sometimes they just wanted to get out of the house. Sometimes their boss "strongly suggested" they take a public speaking class, and your theater happened to be closest to them.

Your job is to suss out who is struggling because improv is genuinely hard for them and who is struggling because they're not even trying. Every student deserves your best coaching, but if someone genuinely isn't trying to get better, you don't want to waste too much energy on them—you'll make yourself crazy.

You should go into every class assuming that all the students are there to learn and grow, but over time, you'll discover who is super motivated to learn, who is just there to have fun, and who is just there because they didn't have anything better to do.

Keep in mind that a student's idea of success may be different from your own. Let go of the idea that every student is going to turn into Wayne Brady. For some people, getting up on stage and having fun is a win. For others, finding a group of people to laugh with is a win. We all want to train the next great generation of improvisers, but that's not every student's goal.

Aim to inspire everyone, but accept that some students are okay with just being okay!

Dealing With "the Know-it-All"

Know-it-alls are tough. They try to side coach other students, debate you every time you give a correction, and are quick to tell you what they used to do in their *other* improv troupe or in someone *else's* class. And they usually won't take a note.

Remember, this is *your* class. Be firm that you will be doing the coaching. Even if they learned something a different way elsewhere, this class is an opportunity for them to learn *your* approach. Getting into lengthy philosophical discussions with know-it-all students wastes everyone's time and undermines your authority. Invite them to chat with you after class, but keep the session moving for everyone's sake.

Teaching Your Peers

Sometimes you will be teaching fellow students, troupe-mates, or even other teachers whose classes you've taken. This can be nerve-wracking and lead to a feeling of imposter syndrome. *They must be judging me!*

Remember, improvisers are naturally kind and supportive. They want you to succeed. If you're in a class with your peers, they're likely proud that you've stepped up to take this next step in your improv journey. When I'm in a class taught by a former student of mine, I can't help but smile, knowing that I played a small part in their growth.

No matter what, *you are the teacher*. Whether the class is twenty strangers or twenty peers, own your authority. Don't defer to more-experienced players or self-deprecate your knowledge. In the event someone helpfully tries to backseat coach, gently let them know you will be doing the coaching today.

After the class, your peers can be a wonderful source for candid feedback. Ask what you did well and what you can improve. View teaching your peers as an opportunity for growth, but don't be afraid to stand in front of them and take control.

Teaching a Full Class Series

This book has focused on teaching individual classes, but you may be called upon to teach an entire class series, such as an eight-week Introduction to Improv. Teaching a class series is mostly just creating individual syllabi for each class (as we've already covered), but there are a few subtle differences to be aware of:

- **Your first class will be front-loaded with administrative and housekeeping items.** There will be introductions, learning names, consent and content discussion, and perhaps a focus on trust-building and getting-to-know-you exercises. You have the luxury of spending more time in your first class on these foundational items, knowing that subsequent classes can get right to the meat of your topic.

- **Each class should begin with a mini recap.** Just as an individual class uses exercises to stack atomic skills atop one another, each class in a series should build upon the previous ones. It can be helpful to start each class with an exercise that reviews the main skill that was learned in the previous class. This exercise can even be the warm-up. Give students a chance to

refresh their memories before diving into new
material.

- **You will get to know each student better.** Over the
course of a class series, you will learn who needs to be
pushed and who needs gentle handling. You will
understand more about each student's individual
skills and limitations. You will also see people make
real progress from beginning to end. Spending a full
class series with a group of students can help you to
build meaningful teacher-student relationships and
effectively customize your teaching to the individuals.

In a full class series, it's even more important to build a sense
of "group mind" and ensemble. This goes beyond just making
sure that everyone knows everyone's names. Add in team
building exercises that build trust and familiarity. Consider
more group games or just-for-fun warm-ups that connect
people. You might also suggest skills students can practice on
their own—encouraging meeting up and building friendships
outside the class. A class series is about learning skills, but it's
also about meeting people, developing friendships, and (hopefully) connecting teammates for the long haul. The number
one thing that brings people back to take more classes isn't the
improv—it's the community.

 *We were asked to give a motivation to another person
and then they go off and do a scene with it. The motivation I gave was, "A fairy that wants to be human."
The improviser proceeded to play the most friendly
and appealing character who desperately wanted to
be a friend to their partner. What I thought was
interesting was how they interpreted "wants to be*

human." It was not taken literally, but rather they saw wanting to be human was a desire for friendship/companionship. That little lesson was really inspiring to me. I learned that wanting to be human can mean lots of things. And people have layers and bring their own biases and perspectives into their scenes.

— Abe Rivera

Chapter 15
Final Thoughts on Getting Started (and Getting Better)

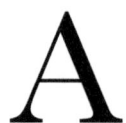re you ready to teach? Great!

So...now what?

If you're lucky, your theater will have a formal teacher training program. In many cases, though, you'll have to find your own way into teaching.

Below are some recommendations.

Make it Known That You Want to Start Teaching

Speak directly to your education director, artistic director, general manager, or whoever schedules teachers and plans classes. Let them know that you're interested in teaching and ask if there's a process for getting started. Tell them you read this book!

It's rare for a theater to have enough teachers. Education directors are often scrambling to fill teaching slots. Lack of good teachers is usually the limiting factor in being able to offer enough classes to meet student demand. Your interest in teaching will likely be greeted with enthusiasm. Most importantly: don't wait to be asked. Stand up and volunteer.

Find Teaching Mentors

Share your interest in teaching with other teachers you respect at your theater. Ask if they will mentor you and allow you to observe their classes. Most teachers will be extremely honored. Ask them questions as you're developing your first classes and invite them to watch you teach and give feedback. Make sure you approach the teachers that you want to be like one day!

You may also want to ask a mentor teacher about co-teaching opportunities. Will they let you assist with teaching a class, perhaps running an exercise or two and helping to develop the syllabus? Once you have more experience, would they let you take the lead while they help where needed? Co-teaching can be a great way to get started in a classroom setting.

Observe Other Classes with a Critical Eye

As you take classes, watch the teacher. How do they manage the class? Do they clearly explain the class thesis at the beginning? Is the progression of exercises clear? Notice if the teacher has broken the end goal into atomic skills, if the energy flags, or if some students get up more than others. What would you do differently? (Note: It's best to keep your observations to yourself, unless the teacher has specifically invited you to give feedback.)

Teach Your First Class!

The best class to start with is something with lower stakes, like a drop-in, your theater's weekly level two rehearsal, or anything with less-experienced students. But don't panic if you're asked to teach something at a higher level. Say yes and trust that you can teach improv (yes, you!).

Just like learning to improvise, learning to teach will be a life-long journey. When you first start, you'll likely do some things well and some things poorly. Take steps to improve your teaching month by month, year by year.

Ask for Feedback

Many theaters do not have a formal (or informal) process for giving feedback to teachers. Make it clear that you're motivated to improve and that you're seeking feedback.

If there is a teacher you know and trust, ask them to attend your class (either as a student or as an observer) and give you feedback afterward. Be clear that you want honest and constructive feedback, not just nice platitudes. Not everyone is good at giving direct, candid feedback. Even if they say, "You were great, I wouldn't change a thing," *insist* that they give you three things you could do better. You can also invite your education director to attend or observe your classes, and remind them that you're seeking critical feedback and improvement.

Asking students for feedback does not always yield helpful results, but it's worth trying. Due to the teacher/student power imbalance, they may not feel comfortable giving you candid criticism, even if it's warranted. Newer students may also not really understand enough about improv or teaching to have useful feedback, other than "I liked this" or "I didn't like this."

But there's no harm in asking! You can either let students know before the class ends that you're open to feedback, or, if your theater doesn't already have a process for gathering anonymous feedback from students, use a service like Suggestion Ox (free for improv teachers and theaters) to gather reviews. Remember to take all in-person student feedback with a grain of salt (you'll probably hear a lot more praise than criticism to your face). If you're truly seeking to improve, you may need to give people an opportunity to share feedback anonymously.

Review What Worked and What Didn't Work in Class

Always review your notes right after class and reflect on what you did well and what could be improved. If you have consistent problem areas, consider discussing them with other teachers in your troupe (or in online groups) for advice.

Give yourself grace for making mistakes. You will *never* perfect your teaching. It's as unpredictable as doing improv—with the added complication of having to manage a roomful of humans. You probably remember improv being difficult and frustrating (and fun) in the beginning; give yourself that same compassion as you learn to teach. I've been teaching for almost twenty-five years, and I still make mistakes all the time.

If you work at it, you *will* get better and you *will* come to love it.

Ask for Help

You do not have to go this alone. There is a large and vibrant online community of improv teachers (see this book's companion site), plus teachers at your theater and within your local community. Whether you need help coming up with a class topic, building a syllabus, choosing the right exercise, or dealing with a tricky student situation, there are kind people ready to help. Improv is a collaborative art, so don't hesitate to ask for help, advice, or encouragement when you need it.

Teach More Often

There's no substitute for the experience gained by getting into the classroom. The more you teach, the better you'll get. Find multiple opportunities to teach so you can put your learnings into practice. "We just have too many teachers," said no theater ever.

Make Your Own Opportunities

You don't have to wait to be asked. If there aren't opportunities at your theater (or there isn't an improv theater in your town), you can set up your own community class at a library, park district, or event space. Everyone needs improv!

Go Teach!

If you're like me, you took your first improv class because it looked like a fun little hobby. You likely didn't know how much improv would change your life by creating dear friends, helping you discover a passion, and showing you an entirely new philosophy for life.

You've surely had the experience of audience members telling you how much they loved a show, how much they needed a laugh, how much what you did on stage made a bad day a little bit better. Improv is a gift you give to others.

Teaching is just like that.

At first, you may want to teach just to give yourself a new challenge or to help out at your theater. Perhaps you have an idea for a class that's been nagging at you. But no matter what your initial motivations are, over time you'll learn the truth: teaching is about changing lives. There are few things more rewarding than watching students have that "light bulb moment," where they are finally able to connect the dots and achieve something on stage that they weren't able to do before. Whether it's a single class, a class series, or your entire career, helping people to discover the joy of improv is profoundly meaningful.

 Carolyn Ramsey dropped this gem on me when I was getting stuck in my scenes: "Don't wait for them to tell you who you are. You tell them who you are." That was so much more than a note for improv class! I felt super seen and it made me more comfortable to just go with whatever I was thinking instead of holding back —on stage and in life.

— Bianca Caban

Once you're an improv teacher, everything changes. You'll never see your shows the same way. You'll have a deeper appreciation for the great improv you watch and a more critical eye for why some scenes, games, and shows are struggling. It will turn you from a one-dimensional player into a multi-dimensional improviser.

Teaching gives you tools to analyze and improve your own performance. It opens doors in the worldwide improv community. Most importantly, teaching will give you more opportunities for fun. Imagine eating but never being able to cook. Imagine listening to music but never being able to sing. Teaching is the piece of your improv puzzle that you didn't even know was missing.

Thank you for reading. Please reach out with your questions and feedback. I'd love to know how this book helps you to become a teacher, and what could be better.

Let's clap it up!

Resources and Cool Stuff

You'll find downloadable worksheets, links to other teaching books, recommended websites and groups, and much more at youcanteachimprov.com.

Acknowledgments

Thanks so much to all the readers who gave feedback on early drafts of this book, including Teylor Burke, Coleman O'Toole, Patrick Short, Rachel Rogers, Kathryn Dionne, Ali Pascale Decker, Ria Torricelli, and Guy Winterbotham.

Jill Bernard gave me invaluable feedback on the manuscript and a generous quote for the cover. Jill was an early inspiration to me as a teacher with her ability to make students feel awesome through the power of "Yay!"

Hadas Cassorla read multiple drafts and gave me the candid feedback I needed. She also makes me go write in the morning.

Ashten Luna Evans copyedited the book to remove some of my more egregious ramblings. The remaining ramblings are my own fault.

Mark Swift's proofreading prevented me from grossly misusing hyphens or omitting the ampersand from Peaches & Herb.

Mark Damon Brooks brought the text to life with a wonderful performance of the audiobook.

And huge thanks to the hundreds of teachers and thousands of students who have challenged and inspired me over the years. Improv is a collaborative art, and all of you helped make this book possible.

About the Author

Andrew Berkowitz is Artistic Director Emeritus at ComedySportz Portland and a teacher and performer at theaters and festivals around the world. He currently lives in Richmond, Virginia, USA, with a dog, two cats, and one girlfriend.

Want teacher training in your city or at your festival? Please reach out. Andrew is portable and loves to travel. Get in touch any time at andrew@andrewberkowitz.com or @andrew-berkowitz on Facebook Messenger.

facebook.com/andrewberkowitz

x.com/andrewberkowitz

linkedin.com/in/andrewberkowitz

goodreads.com/andrewberkowitz

Also by Andrew Berkowitz

Nonfiction

Reffing ComedySportz: The Ultimate Guide to Whistling While You Work

Fiction

Murder and Other Hot Messes: A Charlie Friday Mystery